TEACHING VOCABULARY
Through Differentiated Instruction
With Leveled Graphic Organizers

NANCY L. WITHERELL & MARY C. McMACKIN

NEW YORK • TORONTO • LONDON • AUCKLAND • SYDNEY
MEXICO CITY • NEW DELHI • HONG KONG • BUENOS AIRES

Teaching *Resources*

Dedication

To my three sons: Paul, Jonathan, and TC, who love to ignore my words of wisdom. Love, Mom

To Holly McMackin, whose kind, thoughtful words inspire many. Love, Mary

Editor: Sarah Longhi

Cover design by Maria Lilja

Interior design by Sydney Wright

ISBN-13 978-0-439-89546-0

ISBN-10 0-439-89546-4

2 3 4 5 6 7 8 9 10   40   14 13 12 11 10 09 08 07

Contents

Introduction

"But that's not logical!" a fifth grader proclaimed incredulously while discussing a current novel in reader's workshop. The teacher who overheard the conversation was delighted. *Logical* was a vocabulary word he had spent time teaching a few weeks ago and here it was being used as part of this student's expressive language. A smile danced across the teacher's face. "You just made my day," he thought.

Effective vocabulary instruction takes time, commitment, and resourcefulness, but creating opportunities for students to play with language and watching them increase their word knowledge is also exciting and rewarding. The overviews, model lessons, and graphic organizers in this book help you engage students in meaningful interactions with words they need to know to succeed in language arts and in subjects across the curriculum.

Why Teach Vocabulary?

More than ever the pressure is on to teach vocabulary both explicitly and implicitly. The International Reading Association placed vocabulary on its list of "What's Hot" for 2006, and literacy expert Cathy Collins Block forecasts that vocabulary instruction will be emphasized nationally for the next ten years. Block's research also indicates that a learner needs repeated exposure to a new word to truly learn its meaning. And true ownership of words and a facility with language is the goal of vocabulary instruction.

As you may already know, vocabulary is one of the five main components recommended for reading instruction by the Center for the Improvement of Early Reading Achievement (CIERA), and it has a direct impact on another component—comprehension (McKeown, Beck, Omanson, and Perfetti, 1983). McKeown's research shows how closely vocabulary knowledge and reading achievement are related. She finds that "students with larger vocabularies are more capable readers, and they have a wider repertoire of strategies for figuring out the meanings of unfamiliar words than less

capable readers do" (as cited in Tompkins, 2003, p. 221).

What we've learned about the importance of a strong vocabulary in reading success has pushed teaching vocabulary to the forefront of reading instruction. In the *Handbook of Research on Teaching the English Language Arts* (2003), Baumann, Kame'enui and Ash advise preteaching the vocabulary found in basal readers and textbooks because, "deep, rich levels of word knowledge are needed in order to affect text comprehension" (p. 778).

Recommendations about teaching vocabulary from the National Reading Panel include the following:

❋ vocabulary should be taught both directly and indirectly

❋ repeated exposure to vocabulary items are important

❋ a rich context fosters vocabulary learning

❋ depending on a single vocabulary learning strategy will not yield the best results (NICHD, 2001, p. 4–27)

Clearly, these recommendations require a strong focus on explicit and embedded vocabulary instruction—supported by a variety of helpful strategies and diverse materials—for students to make meaningful and lasting connections with words. And providing those strategies and materials is the aim of this book. The lesson ideas offer word-learning strategies and repeated practice opportunities on three distinct levels so every student can learn at a comfortable and effective pace.

What Words Should We Teach?

Teachers select vocabulary words in different ways. The words you choose to teach might figure prominently in the texts your students are reading; they may connect to a specific discipline; or share a common feature, such as Latin roots; or they might be words your students choose to learn.

Beck, McKeown, and Kucan (2002) have identified three tiers that teachers can use to classify vocabulary words. Tier 1 words are common, everyday words that most elementary and middle school students know and use regularly in speaking and writing, such as *plant, table, run, little,* and *fast.* Tier 2 words are more sophisticated words, often synonyms for more common words students know, such as *immense, modify, abruptly,* and *encounter.* Tier 3 words are words that we come across less frequently. We

often find these words in content-area classes and texts. Words such as *trapezoid, molecules, biome,* and *medieval* are Tier 3 words.

Generally, the high-use Tier 1 words need little reinforcement, if any. Tier 2 words, on the other hand, need to be purposefully taught and reinforced, since they are the foundation of academic language. Students need to interact with many, many Tier 2 words in order to build a strong vocabulary that will help them argue effectively, understand research, and make critical decisions. Tier 3 words, which enable students to understand concepts in social studies, science, health, and other areas, are best taught and reinforced in the specific content areas where they occur, so their meanings can be linked to specific subject matter.

Keep in mind that the context in which a word is used often determines whether it is a Tier 1, Tier 2, or Tier 3 word. For example, *compact* serves as a Tier 2 word when used as a verb, meaning "to pack things together tightly," or as an adjective, meaning "small," as in *compact* car. But, when used in a social studies class to describe an agreement between two groups of people, this same word would be considered a Tier 3 word. Although we have identified some words in this book as Tier 2 or Tier 3 words, keep in mind that words can "live" on more than one tier, depending on the context.

What Does It Mean to Differentiate Instruction With Leveled Graphic Organizers?

When teachers differentiate instruction, they modify the content they deliver, the process of instruction, or the type of product they want students to produce in order to meet the diverse needs of their students. In differentiated vocabulary instruction, teachers often introduce words or build awareness of word parts within a whole-class or small-group setting, so that the words can become part of the group's shared vocabulary. They may model how to use the words in different ways, engage students in conversation about word meanings, show positive and negative examples of correct usage, and so on. Teachers may then have students try out the activity themselves with some teacher guidance. During this process, teachers determine how much support each student will need to successfully complete a follow-up task on his or her own. At this point, teachers are often differentiating their instruction in two

ways: by selecting the *content*—the number or type of words to be learned—and the *product*—the activity that reinforces the ownership of the words.

In the following chapters, you'll find ideas to help you choose the best process for presenting vocabulary or word-learning strategies to students. Then, when students are ready for practice, you'll match each student with the most developmentally appropriate graphic organizer for independent practice. We identify three levels for differentiating your instruction by product:

The *Introductory* level graphic organizers provide students with a great deal of support around the key words/concept introduced in the lesson.

The *Intermediate* level graphic organizers are designed for students who are ready to reinforce and expand their understanding of new vocabulary in slightly more complex ways.

The *Challenging* level graphic organizers are appropriate for students who are capable of elaborating on word meanings and using words in unique, intricate ways. We want to nudge these students to experiment with words and sophisticated concepts.

You may notice that the graphic organizers contain comparable amounts of work. We designed them this way so that students won't be concerned about having more or less work than their peers who are working on different organizers.

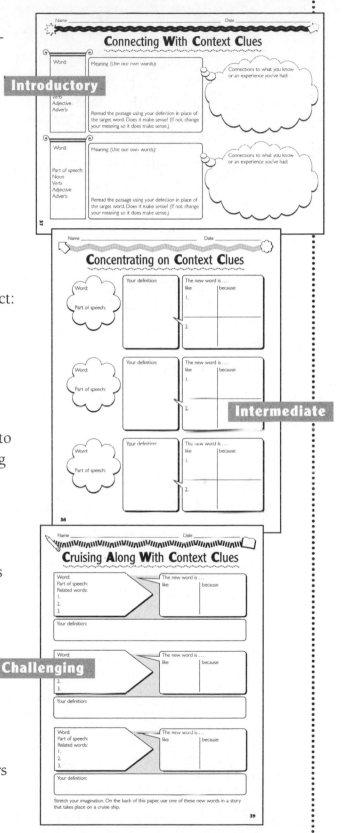

Using the Graphic Organizers Wisely

Students can use tiered graphic organizers independently to reinforce, discover, and clarify meanings, work with word structures, and expand word knowledge. We want to emphasize, however, that the graphic organizers are not ends in themselves. Students should be encouraged to use them to record ideas that they will use again later in a different way. For example, after students have worked independently on different levels of graphic organizers, you might have the entire class share its findings or have small groups work together to compose an advertisement that effectively uses several words they've studied. This culminating step enables students to reinforce what they've learned while absorbing new words and meanings supplied by their peers.

And please, don't think of the graphic organizers in this book as worksheets. They do not specify a limited number of words that we've decided teachers need to teach and students need to learn. Rather, these activities can be returned to again and again to reinforce words that you deem important for your students to learn.

How Do I Get Started?

You can use this book as a supplement to a basal or trade book program or to enhance your own language arts program. The lesson ideas are easy to weave into your reading instruction or across the curriculum. We suggest that you find a chapter that connects to your current instructional focus and try out the model lesson. If you are hesitant about assigning the leveled organizers to different groups for the reinforcement activity, try using the two most appropriate graphic organizers for your students. Remember, there is no one correct way to differentiate instruction for vocabulary. We hope that the resources in this book help you find and fine-tune the best approaches for you to make vocabulary learning more effective and rewarding for your students.

1

Learning New Words

Skill: *Learn new words that are critical to understanding assigned reading passages*

Overview

Although students acquire much of their vocabulary indirectly—through everyday written and spoken activities, such as conversations with friends—they must learn some vocabulary through direct, focused instruction (Adler, 2001). This is especially true when students encounter new words that interfere with their comprehension of a reading assignment. Key words that pose challenges for students either phonetically or semantically should be directly taught to scaffold students' reading experience. Although there are many ways to teach vocabulary directly, most experts agree that when teaching reading vocabulary it is important to have the target words visible, and to use them in a context that students can connect to and remember well.

The model lesson below uses a strategy called "The 8-Step Method"—a focused way to teach new vocabulary explicitly. If you choose not to try this approach, make sure to teach students the meanings of the target words from the assigned reading prior to working with one of the graphic organizers. Keep in mind that current research indicates that students need to hear and work with a new word approximately six times before they are able to remember its meaning (Block, 2005). The graphic organizers in this chapter are designed to help in "cementing" students' understanding of the new word.

How to Teach

The following eight steps are for explicitly teaching and reinforcing vocabulary. The steps are illustrated with examples using the target word *defiant*.

Step 1: Show the word on a word card or highlighted in a list of vocabulary words.

> **defiant**

Tip

You'll want to move through the steps quickly, but not at a rushed pace—the process usually takes about two minutes per word. Introduce a maximum of five to seven words in one period.

Step 2: Have students decode or pronounce the word.

Step 3: Have students guess at a definition and record their ideas on a piece of paper.

Step 4: Show students the word used in context. (This may be a sentence from the assigned text.)

The defiant boy refused to pick up the mess he had made.

Step 5: Have students reconsider the definitions they gave. Ask them to eliminate the ones that no longer make sense in the context of the example sentence, and then use the semantic cues from the sentence to refine the remaining definitions or create a new one. If students have problems with this strategy, guide them. In the above example, ask leading questions such as: what type of boy would make a mess and then refuse to clean it up?

Step 6: Make sure students have the correct definition.

challenging or opposing authority

Step 7: To help students identify the correct use of the word in new contexts, read aloud two sentences that use the word correctly and two that use the word incorrectly. Have students give a thumbs-up if they think the word has been used correctly, and a thumbs-down if the word is used incorrectly.

1. I was defiant *when I did the dishes for Mom.*
   (thumbs-down)

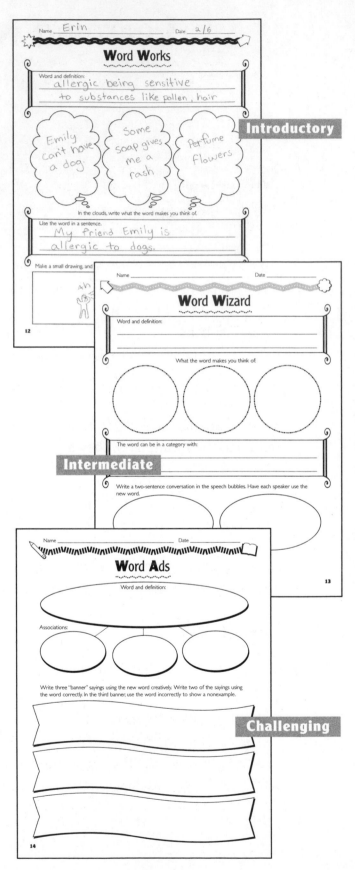

2. The defiant *woman sped angrily out of the room.*
   (thumbs-up)

3. *He was* defiant *when he threw the paper instead of handing it to the clerk.*
   (thumbs-up)

4. *The sweet,* defiant *baby smiled happily at his father.*
   (thumbs-down)

Step 8: Have students create a sentence using the word correctly and share it with a partner (or ask a few volunteers to read their sentences to the group). Ask partners (or the group) to provide feedback so that students can, if necessary, revise their sentences to best reflect the word's meaning.

Step 9 (optional): Discuss derivatives of the word.

   defying, defiance, defiantly, defiantness, defy, defies, defied

Do the 8-Step Method with each word. By the eighth step, students should know the word well enough to complete a graphic organizer successfully.

Using the Tiered Organizers

When students have begun to learn the new word(s) and need practice to reinforce the meaning(s), they are ready for one of the following graphic organizers. (Note: If students need more support, you may want to keep the words and definitions visible as they work on the organizers.)

Introductory: **Word Works**
Students reinforce their understanding of a word's meaning by writing the word and its definition, making associations, using the word in a sentence and making a drawing of the word in action.

Intermediate: **Word Wizard**
Students reinforce their understanding of a word's meaning by writing the word and its definition, making associations and categorizing, and using it in two sentences that form a dialogue.

Challenging: **Word Ads**
Students reinforce their understanding of a word's meaning by writing the word and its definition, making associations, and using the word in three "banner" statements (two statements must give an example of what the word means, the third must give a "nonexample" to show what the word is not).

Word Works

Word and definition:

_____

_____

In the clouds, write what the word makes you think of.

Use the word in a sentence.

_____

_____

Make a small drawing, and show the word in action or being used in some way.

Word Wizard

Word and definition:

_____

_____

What the word makes you think of:

The word can be in a category with:

_____

_____

Write a two-sentence conversation in the speech bubbles. Have each speaker use the new word.

Word Ads

Word and definition:

Associations:

Write three "banner" sayings using the new word creatively. Write two of the sayings using the word correctly. In the third banner, use the word incorrectly to show a nonexample.

Polysemantic Words

Skill: *Recognize that a word can have multiple meanings, depending on the context in which it is used.*

Overview

Our language is full of words that have multiple, diverse meanings—some, like *position*, have ten or more distinct definitions. To help students navigate texts effectively, we need to teach them to be alert to the possibility that a word can be defined in different ways. This is particularly important in content-area reading, where students often encounter familiar words used in new ways. For example, *legend* usually means a story handed down through generations, but in the context of a map unit, *legend* refers to an explanatory list of symbols.

How to Teach

Drawing from texts your students are reading, record on chart paper one or two sentences that contain polysemantic words. For example, you might display the following sentence from page 85 of Gary Paulsen's *Hatchet*: "Not twenty feet to his right, leaning out over the water were birches, and he stood looking at them for a full half-minute before they registered on his mind." Elicit from students as many different definitions for *register* as they can give you and record their responses on the chart paper, under the sentence. Students might know *register* as a noun (a machine in which store clerks keep money), or as a verb (to have your name placed on a list—for example, a list of eligible voters). In this model sentence, however, neither definition fits. Ask students if they can come up with a synonym for "registered" that works in this sentence. (They may tell you "popped into" or "made an impression on.") Let students use a dictionary to find other meanings for *register*, as well. They may be surprised to find more than four! Discuss less common definitions for your target words, when appropriate, and add them to your chart.

Confusion might also arise when students encounter the word *occupation* in the book *Number the Stars*. For many students, *occupation* means a person's job. In Lois Lowry's book, however, *occupation* refers to the Nazis taking control of Denmark in 1940. Explain that in some cases, readers can determine meanings of words by looking at the base word. This is the case with *occupation* (to occupy). Other times, we must use context to find meaning.

Model how to complete the graphic organizers for polysemantic words using a target word (*scale* is the example used here). First, make a three-column chart and place it where everyone can see it. In the first column, which can be

narrower than the other two, write *scale*. In the middle column, record as many definitions as students can generate for *scale*. Next, have students think about each definition and suggest a person who might use the word with that definition. Your completed chart might look something like this:

Word	Meanings	Who would use it?
scale	1. musical notes in a sequence 2. an instrument to measure weight 3. to climb 4. a line mark on a map that indicates distance 5. protective covering of fish	1. a piano teacher 2. someone on a diet 3. a person who climbs rocks 4. travelers who want to know how long it will take to get places 5. a fish market owner

Finally, use the following sentence to model how the same word (or a derivative of it) can be used in two different ways within one sentence: *The bathroom scale showed that Annette lost five pounds after scaling Mt. Frederickson last weekend.*

Pass out a short text and have students locate polysemantic words. Repeat the process described above using a few of the words they find.

Here are some additional polysemantic words that might be useful to students who need some more instruction before working on the graphic organizers:

Word	Meanings
channel	1. a TV frequency (noun) 2. to direct into a certain path (verb) 3. a waterway (noun students might see in content areas)
pound	1. 16 ounces (noun) 2. a place where stray animals are kept (noun) 3. to crush by beating (verb) 4. slang for money (noun)
compact	1. a small case to put cosmetics (noun) 2. solid or packed together tightly (adjective) 3. to compress (verb) 4. an agreement (noun students might see in social studies)

Using the Tiered Organizers

Once students can identify polysemantic words while reading, determine the most appropriate tiered activity for each student. (You or your students may select words.)

Introductory: **Drawing on Knowledge (not the walls)**
Students identify three polysemantic words from their reading, indicate where they are located, and provide two different meanings for each word.

Intermediate: **Lots of Meanings (not parking lots)**
Students identify three polysemantic words from their reading, indicate where the words are found, and provide three different meanings for each word. Students also specify who would use the word in each instance.

Challenging: **Common and Rare Words (not meat)**
Students identify three polysemantic words from their reading, indicate where the words are found, and provide up to four different meanings for each word. Then they compose a sentence using one polysemantic word to convey two distinct meanings.

Drawing on Knowledge (not the walls)

Word:

_____

Where did you find the word?

_____

_____

_____

Meaning:

_____

_____

_____

_____

_____

Another meaning:

_____

_____

_____

_____

_____

Word:

_____

Where did you find the word?

_____

_____

_____

Meaning:

_____

_____

_____

_____

_____

Another meaning:

_____

_____

_____

_____

_____

Word:

_____

Where did you find the word?

_____

_____

_____

Meaning:

_____

_____

_____

_____

Another meaning:

_____

_____

_____

_____

Name _____   Date _____

Lots of Meanings (not parking lots)

Word	**Meanings**	**Who would use it?**
Where did you find the word?	1. _____ _____ 2. _____ _____ 3. _____ _____	1. _____ 2. _____ 3. _____
Word	**Meanings**	**Who would use it?**
Where did you find the word?	1. _____ _____ 2. _____ _____ 3. _____ _____	1. _____ 2. _____ 3. _____
Word	**Meanings**	**Who would use it?**
Where did you find the word?	1. _____ _____ 2. _____ _____ 3. _____ _____	1. _____ 2. _____ 3. _____

Common and Rare Words (not meat)

Word	Meanings

Where did you find the word?

1. _____
2. _____
3. _____
4. _____

Sentence (use the word twice in the same sentence to show two different meanings):

Word	Meanings

Where did you find the word?

1. _____
2. _____
3. _____
4. _____

Sentence (use the word twice in the same sentence to show two different meanings):

Word	Meanings

Where did you find the word?

1. _____
2. _____
3. _____
4. _____

Sentence (use the word twice in the same sentence to show two different meanings):

Enriching Vocabulary

Skill: *Enlarge and enrich vocabulary by discovering new, interesting, and unusual words.*

Overview

To build a strong vocabulary, students must actively acquire new words that they encounter in narrative texts, content-area reading, and unusual sources. Our vocabulary instruction must encourage students to tune in to new and interesting words that increase their reading comprehension and communication skills, as well as their appreciation and enjoyment of words. We need to make a habit out of identifying reading materials that include new and interesting words to supplement students' incidental word learning.

Some vocabulary-enriching sources you may want to have in your classroom include the following:

- a variety of maps—labeled with natural resources, endangered species, or topography notations

- travel brochures filled with enticing, descriptive words

- direction booklets for a wide range of appliances (these provide useful examples of specialized vocabulary, along with challenging text structure).

- paint swatches from home improvement stores that give precise color tones, descriptive words associated with colors, and alliterative language such as *passion pink*, *amazing maize*, and *scintillating cinnabar*

- cereal boxes, comic strips, menus, and even telephone book advertisements that attract students' attention and are loaded with Tier 2 and Tier 3 words.

Keep a wide variety of classroom reading materials available for independent reading. By displaying items like brochures, comic strips, and maps in a prominent place, you can entice students to read and absorb the vocabulary on their own.

It is also a good idea to seek out books that offer myriad and unusual vocabulary words for students. *Slowly, Slowly, Slowly Said the Sloth* (Carle, 2002) uses unusual terms to describe movement, and has picture support for struggling readers or English language learners at this level. *Miss Alaineus, A Vocabulary*

Disaster (Frasier, 2000) is heavily laden with rich words, both in the story line and in alphabetical sentences on each page. Also, any book in the *Series of Unfortunate Events* (Lemony Snicket, 2004) collection is chock-full of robust vocabulary, including definitions— a device through which the author develops his distinct voice.

How to Teach

Prior to the lesson, select vocabulary-rich materials to use with the class. The idea is to set up a vocabulary-rich read, so students can self-select vocabulary words. The materials you choose should contain unusual and challenging words in order to expose students to vocabulary beyond their ordinary experience. Materials may include a section of an owner's manual for an MP3 player (or another hi-tech device), articles from news magazines written for students, such as *Scholastic News*, or texts that students are currently reading, selected for this purpose.

Have students quietly read the material aloud with a partner or in small groups and then select five words that they find interesting or unusual. Model for students how you would select a word and guess at its meaning. Use this word in a phrase or sentence that you could put on a poster as a caption or comment.

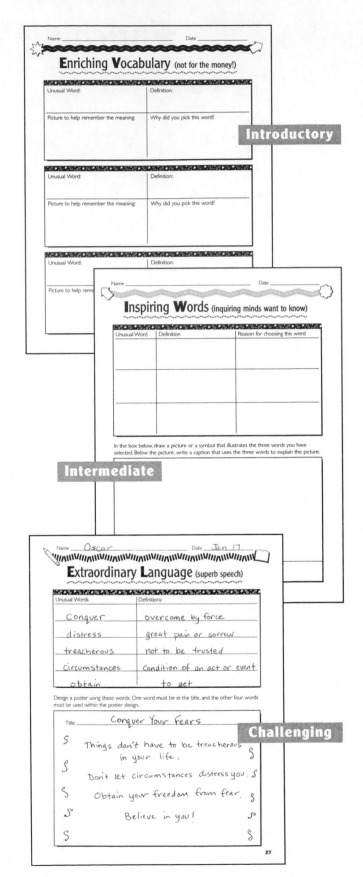

Have students use copies of the T-chart provided on page 24, or they can draw their own, to organize their words. It's important that students each fill out a T-chart because later they will complete separate, and perhaps different, leveled graphic organizers. Have students write each word on the T-chart, and guess at its meaning from context. As students select words, walk around and "check in" with groups. After students have selected their words, ask three or four groups to share their guesses with the class. Finally, have students use dictionaries to check their accuracy.

Using the Tiered Organizers

The following graphic organizers are appropriate for students who can choose interesting and unusual words to study, and can give reasons for their selections. Students first use the T-chart to work together to select words and predict meaning from context. Then they look up the word in the dictionary to confirm their predictions or refine the definition, if necessary, and they complete one of the following graphic organizers.

Introductory: **Enriching Vocabulary (not for the money!)**
Students select and write three vocabulary words, and then write a definition for each word. Next, students draw a graphic for each word and explain their selections.

Intermediate: **Inspiring Words (inquiring minds want to know)**
Students select and write three vocabulary words, write definitions, and explain their selections. They then draw a picture that relates to all three words, along with an appropriate caption using each vocabulary word.

Challenging: **Extraordinary Language (superb speech)**
Students select and write five vocabulary words and their definitions, and then design a poster that includes these words. At least one word must be used in the title, and the other four should be part of the design of the poster.

Enriching Vocabulary T-Chart

As you read, select five interesting or unusual words from the reading material. Fill in the T-Chart, writing the words on one side, and what you think the words might mean on the other side.

Unusual words	What the words might mean

Enriching Vocabulary (not for the money!)

Unusual Word:	Definition:
Picture to help remember the meaning:	Why did you pick this word?

Unusual Word:	Definition:
Picture to help remember the meaning:	Why did you pick this word?

Unusual Word:	Definition:
Picture to help remember the meaning:	Why did you pick this word?

Inspiring Words (inquiring minds want to know)

Unusual Word	Definition	Reason for choosing this word

In the box below, draw a picture or a symbol that illustrates the three words you have selected. Below the picture, write a caption that uses the three words to explain the picture.

Extraordinary Language (superb speech)

Unusual Word	Definition

Design a poster using these words. One word must be in the title, and the other four words must be used within the poster design.

Title _____

Self-Selected **V**ocabulary

Skill: *Claim ownership of interesting and challenging word*

Overview

Another way to help enrich students' vocabularies is to encourage them
to lay claim to words that they find interesting, important, intriguing, or
confusing. It's highly motivating for students to feel a sense of ownership of
words, especially words they can incorporate into their personal word lists.

How to Teach

On an overhead, copy a passage from a text you are reading, perhaps a
newspaper article that contains a word you've never seen before, or have
seen but do not completely understand. Explain why you are interested in
learning this word. Tell students you want to "own" the word. Model how
you use strategies to determine the word's meaning: using context cues,
checking for roots or affixes, and/or consulting a dictionary. Share with
students other words that come from the same base word (related words).
After determining the word's meaning and confirming it with a dictionary,
make a list of associations or synonyms that could help you remember—
and own—the meaning of the target word. Model how to refer to a
thesaurus for ideas. Repeat this process with a different word.

   Next, give each student (or partners) a few minutes to search texts
that they are reading (or that you have assigned) for unfamiliar words they
would like to own. Ask for volunteers to share a few of these words and
read them in the context of the surrounding sentence or sentences. Invite
volunteers to explain why they chose these words and how they might
discover the words' meanings. Finally, have them offer associations or words
with similar meanings to help connect the new word with information they
already know.

   On a white erase board, create a chart to record new words,
definitions, and synonyms. After several students share, take a few words

and model how you might use the word creatively in a simile. Finally, get students involved in creating similes with their words. Your chart might look like this:

Word	Definition	Synonyms	Simile
reliable (to rely, reliability)	can count on to do what is expected and correct	dependable, trustworthy, accurate, responsible	as reliable as a beating heart
reluctant (reluctance, reluctantly)	not eager or willing to do something	uncooperative, opposed, unwilling	as reluctant as a miser to part with his money
surplus	what remains after all that was needed or used is gone	extra, additional, unnecessary	as unappetizing as surplus potato salad left in the hot sun after a picnic

Using the Tiered Organizers

Once students can select appropriate Tier 2 or Tier 3 words to learn and can demonstrate strategies for determining word meaning, match students with tiered graphic organizers. After students complete graphic organizers, have them come together to share their "owned" words and new ways of conceptualizing them.

Introductory: **Framing Fascinating Words**
Students find two words they would like to learn, place each word in a frame, and write the definition below the word. Next, they write synonyms around the perimeter of the frame, and decorate it.

Intermediate: **Clouds of Colorful Words**
Students find two words they would like to learn, place each word in a box, and write the definition below the word. Next, they write synonyms and words that share the same base word as the vocabulary word, to create strong associations.

Challenging: **Special Words and Similes**

Students find two words they would like to learn, and place each word and its definition in the oval. Students write related words and synonyms around the oval. Finally, they write a simile, using the target word.

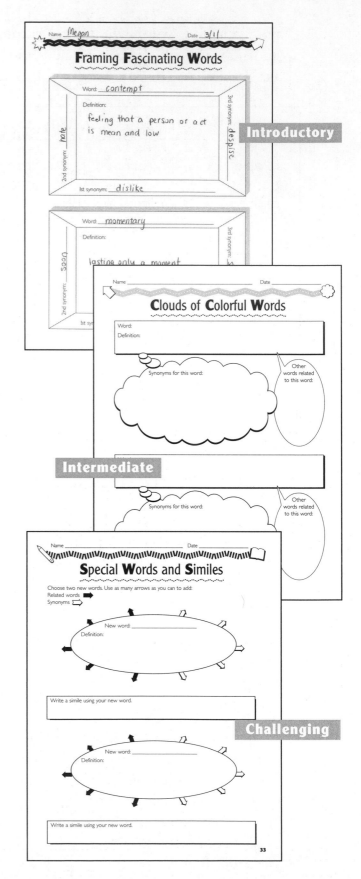

Name Megan   Date 3/1

Framing Fascinating Words

Word: contempt

Definition:
feeling that a person or act is mean and low

2nd synonym: hate

3rd synonym: despise

1st synonym: dislike

Introductory

Word: momentary

Definition:
lasting only a moment

2nd synonym: soon

3rd synonym:

1st sy

Name   Date

Clouds of Colorful Words

Word:
Definition:

Synonyms for this word:

Other words related to this word:

Intermediate

Synonyms for this word:

Other words related to this word:

Name   Date

Special Words and Similes

Choose two new words. Use as many arrows as you can to add:
Related words ▶
Synonyms ▷

New word: _____
Definition:

Write a simile using your new word.

Challenging

New word: _____
Definition:

Write a simile using your new word.

33

Framing Fascinating Words

Word: _____

Definition:

3rd synonym: _____

2nd synonym: _____

1st synonym: _____

Word: _____

Definition:

3rd synonym: _____

2nd synonym: _____

1st synonym: _____

Clouds of Colorful Words

Word:

Definition:

Synonyms for this word:

Other words related to this word:

Word:

Definition:

Synonyms for this word:

Other words related to this word:

Special Words and Similes

Choose two new words. Use as many arrows as you can to add:

Related words ➡

Synonyms ⇨

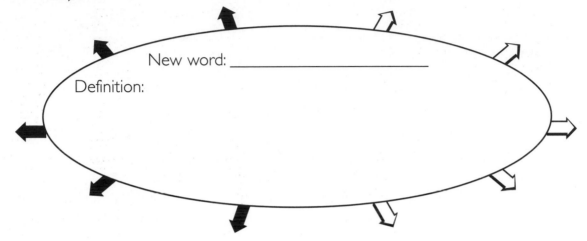

New word: _____

Definition:

Write a simile using your new word.

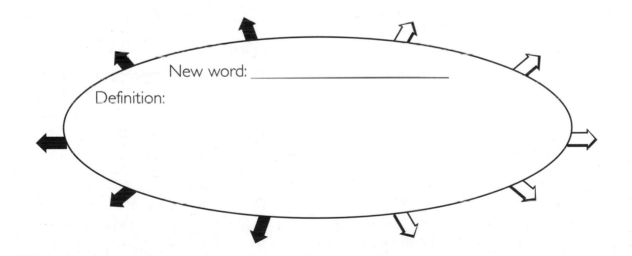

New word: _____

Definition:

Write a simile using your new word.

5

Vocabulary in Context

Skill: *Use words surrounding an unfamiliar word to determine its meaning*

Overview

It's been reported that students learn about 2,000 to 3,000 new words per year. They learn many of these words from direct instruction, but many more from the variety of reading they do. Often, word meaning can be gleaned by focusing on surrounding words and sentences, or context. When using context clues, it's important to remember that the word's definition is limited to this one context; readers with strong vocabularies are able to substitute synonyms for unknown words and to extend the meaning of a known word to other contexts.

How to Teach

Select a few target words from an engaging text your students are reading, such as *Holes* by Louis Sachar (1998). You may decide that *perseverance*, a word used on page 8, would be an important Tier 2 word for students. Many characters in this book, as well as in other texts, show perseverance, often in the face of adversity.

Using an overhead transparency, copy the paragraph in which the target word appears. Read the paragraph aloud, pointing out the target word. Explain that sometimes authors provide clues to help readers figure out unfamiliar words. In the *perseverance* example, you might read the paragraph and note that the author uses the word when he mentions that Stanley's father would work on a job for years—sometimes going without sleep for days.

Discuss parts of speech and how knowing a word's part of speech can offer clues to its meaning. If, for example, we can determine from the sentence that the target word is a verb, we know that it's describing some type of action. If it's an adjective, it would describe a noun or pronoun. Sachar uses the word *perseverance* in the following sentence: "Stanley's father was smart and had a lot of perseverance" (p.8).

Because *perseverance* is a noun, we know that it refers to a person, place, thing, or quality. Explain that *perseverance* refers to a quality.

Next, show students how to define the target word in their own words and reread the passage, substituting a definition that you provide in the paragraph. You might say, for example, "Stanley's father was smart and showed everyone that he would work hard to accomplish what he set out to do." Model asking yourself, "Does it make sense?"

Introduce students to words related to your target word, too, like *persevere*. Since words that are built from a common base word have similar meanings, learning one word can often help us learn many other semantically related words. Have students explain how the target word (or a related word) connects to something in their lives, then talk about how the target word is like other, more familiar words (*determination*, *patience*, and *persistence*). You might point out that people who show a great deal of perseverance also tend to show determination (they don't give up), patience (they are willing to keep trying even if it takes a while), and persistence (they move steadily along).

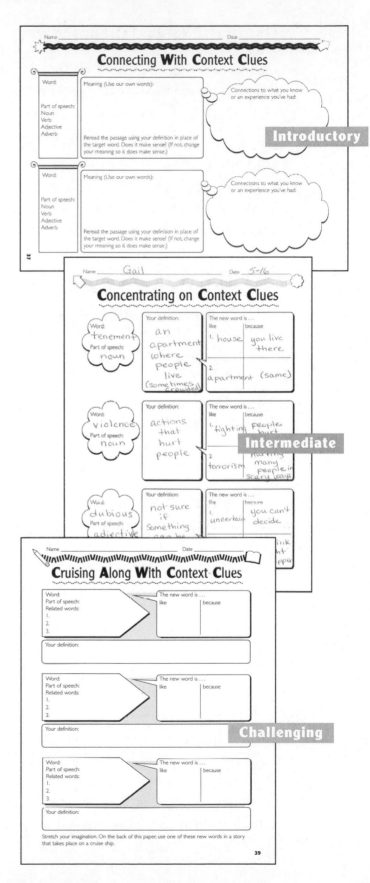

Using the Tiered Organizers

Before matching students with tiered graphic organizers, check to see that they can use context clues to determine the meaning of unfamiliar words, identify parts of speech, and compare words with similar meanings.

Introductory: **Connecting With Context Clues**

Students identify (or you may assign) two unfamiliar words from their reading. They determine each word's part of speech and write its meaning in their own words. Next, they reread the passage, substituting their own definitions and checking that the definition makes sense. Finally, they explain how these words connect to their prior knowledge or experiences.

Intermediate: **Concentrating on Context Clues**

Students identify (or you may assign) three unfamiliar words from their reading. They record each word's part of speech and write its meaning in their own words. Last, students list two words that have similar but slightly different meanings and explain how the words are similar in meaning and/or usage.

Challenging: **Cruising Along With Context Clues**

Students identify (or you may assign) three unfamiliar words from their reading, record each word's part of speech, and list up to three other words that are related to it. They define each target word, provide a word that has a similar but slightly different meaning, and explain why these words are similar. Finally, they stretch their imaginations by writing a short story using one of the target words. The story should take place on a cruise ship.

Connecting With Context Clues

Word: _____

Part of speech:
Noun
Verb
Adjective
Adverb

Meaning (Use our own words):

Reread the passage using your definition in place of the target word. Does it make sense? (If not, change your meaning so it does make sense.)

Connections to what you know or an experience you've had:

Word: _____

Part of speech:
Noun
Verb
Adjective
Adverb

Meaning (Use our own words):

Reread the passage using your definition in place of the target word. Does it make sense? (If not, change your meaning so it does make sense.)

Connections to what you know or an experience you've had:

Concentrating on Context Clues

Word:

Part of speech:

Your definition:

The new word is . . .

like	because
1.	
2.	

Word:

Part of speech:

Your definition:

The new word is . . .

like	because
1.	
2.	

Word:

Part of speech:

Your definition:

The new word is . . .

like	because
1.	
2.	

Cruising Along With Context Clues

Word:
Part of speech:
Related words:
1.
2.
3.

The new word is . . .

like	because

Your definition:

Word:
Part of speech:
Related words:
1.
2.
3.

The new word is . . .

like	because

Your definition:

Word:
Part of speech:
Related words:
1.
2.
3.

The new word is . . .

like	because

Your definition:

Stretch your imagination. On the back of this paper, use one of these new words in a story that takes place on a cruise ship.

Academic Language

Skill: Understand "school talk"—essential vocabulary used in the content areas as well as words that signal important functions of language across all content areas

Overview

We expect students to communicate in school with a much richer vocabulary than they use in their daily conversations. Some of the "academic" words we want them to use are more sophisticated expressions that help to clarify their thinking. Across content areas, for example, we give instructions using words that describe language functions such as *persuade*, *describe*, and *categorize*. Other school-related terms students must learn are discipline-specific, such as *divisor* (mathematics). And many words serve both purposes. In science or in a debate, for example, we could use *hypothesize* and *interpret*. Students need to regularly acquire and use these academic and content-area words (Tier 2 and Tier 3 words) in order to be successful in school.

How to Teach

In this lesson, we focus on vocabulary that signals language function, but you may choose some other type of academic language for this lesson. We have chosen to use the words in the model lesson because students will encounter them across grades and academic subjects and in both reading and writing. We use text messaging—a popular method by which students communicate—to bridge the gap between familiar language and less-familiar academic language.

To begin, list the following four terms down the left side of a piece of chart paper: *explain*, *evaluate*, *analyze*, and *synthesize*. Next, have students brainstorm how they would define each term and record their responses to the right of each term. Your chart should look like this:

explain	
evaluate	
analyze	
synthesize	

Discuss how academic language is similar to text messaging. For example, you can state that each text message communicates ideas, that people use different vocabulary to communicate in various settings, and so on. Distribute a list of school-appropriate text message abbreviations, such as:

AFAIK	As far as I know	IAC	In any case
B4	Before	IC	I see
CMIIW	Correct me if I'm wrong	IIRC	If I remember correctly
NE1	Anyone	IDK	I don't know
PROLLY	Probably	IMHO	In my humble opinion
GB	Goodbye	IMO	In my opinion
SOL	Sooner or later	IOW	In other words
KNIM	Know what I mean?	JIC	Just in case

Return to your chart. Have students help you rewrite one of the definitions as it might be written in a text message. For instance, a text message used to define *explain* might be "IIRC explain MENS 2GIVDTLO2K," meaning, "If I remember correctly, explain means to give details or to clarify." Encourage students to supply text-message abbreviations for the rest of the definitions in the chart. Then have students work with partners or in small groups to brainstorm school subjects and situations in which they might hear or see each term used.

Using the Tiered Organizers

When students are comfortable using text-message abbreviations as described above, match them to the appropriate tiered activity. Before assigning the challenging graphic organizer, review common dictionary abbreviations (for example, parts of speech and abbreviations used in etymologies) with students who will be completing this organizer.

Introductory: **Text Messaging Meanings**

Students write and define two academic terms and then compose a text message in which they explain each word's meaning and then translate the text message into Standard English.

Intermediate: **Translating School Terminology**

Students write and define two academic terms and then compose a text message in which they explain each word's meaning. Once they translate the text message into Standard English, students identify a school subject in which the term might be used.

Challenging: **Abbreviations Here, There, and Everywhere**

Students write two academic terms and then look up each one in a dictionary (or dictionaries). They then compose two text messages: one explaining the word's meaning in their own words, the other containing information about etymology (word origins), part of speech, or related words, or providing alternate definitions. Finally, students translate their text messages into Standard English.

(Note: If students aren't familiar with the term *etymology*, you might want to review Chapter 13, which focuses on word origins, before assigning this activity.)

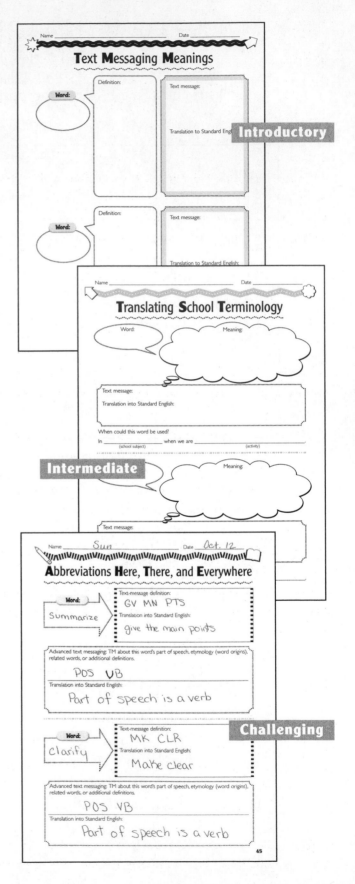

Text Messaging Meanings

Word:

Definition:

Text message:

Translation to Standard English:

Word:

Definition:

Text message:

Translation to Standard English:

Translating School Terminology

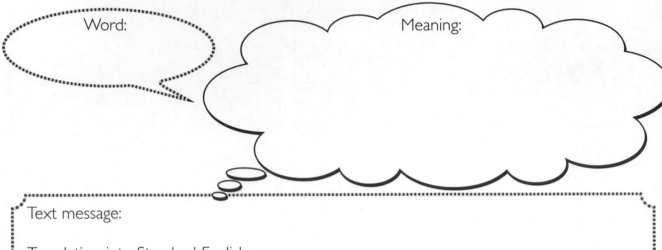

Word:

Meaning:

Text message:

Translation into Standard English:

When could this word be used?

In _____ when we are _____.
      (school subject)   (activity)

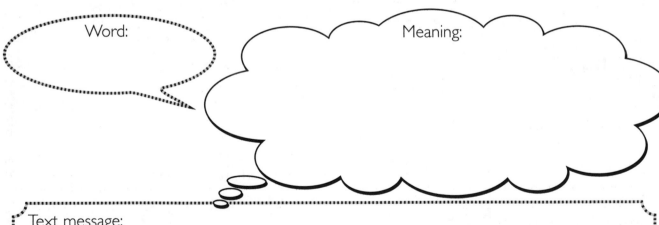

Word:

Meaning:

Text message:

Translation into Standard English:

When could this word be used?

In _____ when we are _____.
      (school subject)   (activity)

Abbreviations Here, There, and Everywhere

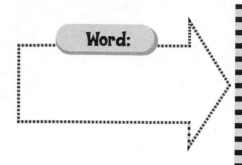

Text-message definition:

Translation into Standard English:

Advanced text messaging: TM about this word's part of speech, etymology (word origins), related words, or additional definitions.

_____

Translation into Standard English:

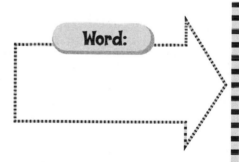

Text-message definition:

Translation into Standard English:

Advanced text messaging: TM about this word's part of speech, etymology (word origins), related words, or additional definitions.

_____

Translation into Standard English:

Incidental Word Learning

Skill: *Grasp word meaning through repeated, casual exposure to words*

Overview

The word *incidental* means "incurred casually," and that is exactly what happens with incidental word learning. We encounter a new word numerous times, and eventually come to understand its meaning by using contextual clues in the surrounding sentence or passage. Learning words this way usually requires at least a few encounters with the new word, since a single sentence or passage usually does not provide enough clues. Over time, as we collect hints at the word's meaning, we eventually get the gist of it. As an analogy, think of a young child learning the word *wet*. The diaper is wet, the floor is wet, Mom's hands are wet. No one takes the child's hand and says, "Here, feel *dry*, now feel *wet*." Yet, it is continual exposure to the spoken word and the experience that helps the child eventually understand *wet*. This same phenomenon occurs when children read; as they casually encounter quasi-familiar words, they eventually find meaning.

How to Teach

The purpose of using graphic organizers in this chapter is not to teach vocabulary, but to aid students in honing in on the exact meaning of words they casually encounter. In the lesson offered here, sentences include words that students may have heard before, but may not completely understand.

Begin with pairs of sentences, such as those listed on page 47, that include ample context to help students infer word meaning. Write the sentence pairs on the board, underlining the unfamiliar words. Ask students to use the context of the sentences to define the underlined words in their own language. When discussing the words, have students offer other examples of how the word can be used in a sentence and how it may *not* be used in a sentence (a nonexample).

Pair 1

The usually patient man was piqued because he had to stand in line so long.

Angela could tell by her mother's irritated expression that she was piqued about something.

Pair 2

Gail was adamant that she could get the project done on time and we were not to worry.

John was adamant that his son would not go on the dangerous rafting trip.

Pair 3

The shoes with shiny beads were very sophisticated for such a young girl.

Samantha impressed everyone with her knowledgeable and sophisticated answer.

Using the Tiered Organizers

When students can infer meanings for words that they have seen before but do not completely understand, they are ready for one of the following graphic organizers.

Introductory: **It Means What?**
Students identify two words in their reading that they do not completely understand, guess at

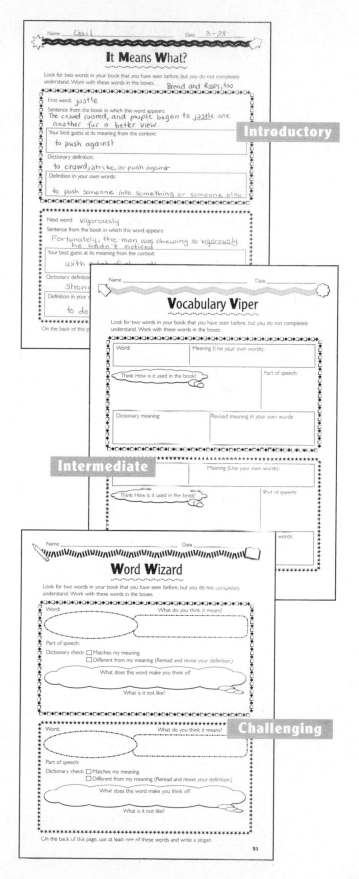

the meanings, and then look up the meanings in the dictionary. Students then write each word artistically to show its meaning.

Intermediate: **Vocabulary Viper**

Students identify two words in their reading that they do not completely understand and guess at the meanings. They record how the words are used in the book and their parts of speech, then they look up the meanings in a dictionary. Students write a definition in their own words and use one of the words in a sentence.

Challenging: **Word Wizard**

Students identify two words in their reading that they do not completely understand, guess at the meanings and record their parts of speech. Students check to see if their definitions resemble a dictionary definition and make associations to help them recall the meanings. They give a nonexample for each word and write a slogan using at least one of the words.

It Means What?

Look for two words in your book that you have seen before, but you do not completely understand. Work with these words in the boxes.

First word:

Sentence from the book in which this word appears:

Your best guess at its meaning from the context:

Dictionary definition:

Definition in your own words:

Next word:

Sentence from the book in which this word appears:

Your best guess at its meaning from the context:

Dictionary definition:

Definition in your own words:

On the back of this page, write one of the words artistically to show its meaning.

Vocabulary Viper

Look for two words in your book that you have seen before, but you do not completely understand. Work with these words in the boxes.

Word: | Meaning (Use your own words):

Think: How is it used in the book?

Part of speech:

Dictionary meaning: | Revised meaning in your own words:

Word: | Meaning (Use your own words):

Think: How is it used in the book?

Part of speech:

Dictionary meaning: | Revised meaning in your own words:

On the back of this page, write a sentence using one of the words.

Word Wizard

Look for two words in your book that you have seen before, but you do not completely understand. Work with these words in the boxes.

Word:

What do you think it means?

Part of speech:

Dictionary check: ☐ Matches my meaning

☐ Different from my meaning (Reread and revise your definition.)

What does this word make you think of?

What is it not like?

Word:

What do you think it means?

Part of speech:

Dictionary check: ☐ Matches my meaning

☐ Different from my meaning (Reread and revise your definition.)

What does this word make you think of?

What is it not like?

On the back of this page, use at least one of these words and write a slogan.

Reinforcing Content-Area Vocabulary

Skill: *Enrich understanding of content-area word meanings by sorting words into categories*

Overview

This model lesson helps students deepen their understanding of content-area vocabulary words through the process of sorting, using categories students choose themselves. The words, which may come from a unifying theme or topic, such as voting rights or weather, are Tier 3 words, such as *suffrage* (social studies) and *cumulus* (science), which occur much less frequently than Tier 1 and Tier 2 words.

This activity provides repeated exposure to the content-area meanings of the selected words, allowing students to build associations that make those meanings "stick." In order for students to categorize words correctly, they must think about the meanings of the words. They also must read and reread words to gain word fluency. As they sort, students begin to realize that words often fall into multiple categories, and this process of evaluating and regrouping increases the number of associations that they make with the target words.

How to Teach

To introduce word sorting, read the target words aloud and describe your process as you determine categories into which they might be sorted, then sort words into appropriate categories. Start with familiar words until students are comfortable with this activity, then have them use content-area words, as in the model lesson that follows.

Let's begin with a sample lesson for a social studies unit on feudalism and the Middle Ages. By the end of the first week, you have introduced the term *feudalism* and have taught the following words related to feudalism:

abbey	knight	monk	steward
armor	lord	peasant	squire
crusades	manor	serf	vassal

The following day, engage your students in word sorts to reinforce their understanding. To model word sorts, write each word on an individual flash card, or if you're using an overhead, write all the words on a transparency and cut it into individual slips with one word on each.

You might group the words as follows and display them for the class:

1. *abbey* and *manor*. Label these "words that signify places"

2. *armor* and *crusades*. Label these "words that relate to battles"

3. *knight, lord, monk, peasant, serf, steward, squire,* and *vassals*. Label these "words that identify people"

Point out to students that there is no one right way to categorize these words. To demonstrate this, regroup the words as follows:

1. *monk* and *abbey*. Label these "words that relate to religion"

2. *armor, crusades, knight, squire,* and *manor*. Label these "words that relate to warriors"

3. *lord, peasant, serf, steward,* and *vassal*. Label these "words that connect the lord and his land"

Ask students to work in small groups or with partners to categorize the words in at least one other way.

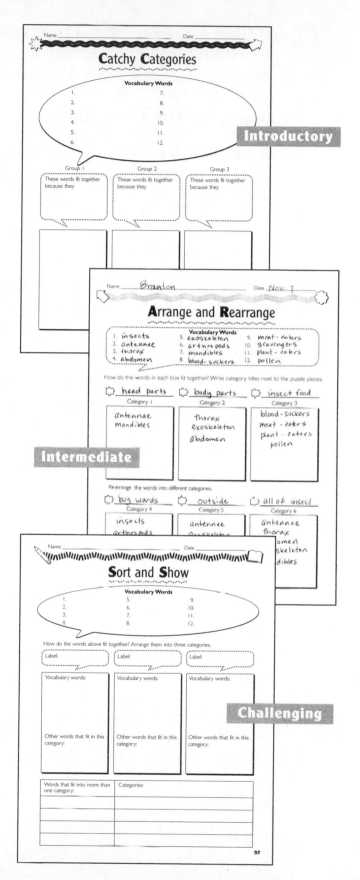

To recap, have students share how they categorized the words. Review what students have learned about each word and ensure that they have an accurate definition for each one.

Using the Tiered Organizers

Match students to graphic organizers when they understand how to sort words into multiple categories.

Introductory: **Catchy Categories**
Students sort teacher-designated vocabulary words into groups related by meanings, and then label each group.

Intermediate: **Arrange and Rearrange**
Students sort teacher-designated vocabulary words into groups related by meaning and then label each group. Next, they repeat this process, finding a different way to sort and label the same words.

Challenging: **Sort and Show**
Students sort teacher-designated vocabulary words into groups related by meaning and then label each group. They include an additional word of their own choosing in each category. Finally, students list words that fit into more than one category and specify the categories.

Catchy Categories

Vocabulary Words

1.   7.
2.   8.
3.   9.
4.   10.
5.   11.
6.   12.

Group 1

These words fit together because they

Group 2

These words fit together because they

Group 3

These words fit together because they

Arrange and **R**earrange

Vocabulary Words

1.   5.   9.
2.   6.   10.
3.   7.   11.
4.   8.   12.

How do the words in each box fit together? Write category titles next to the puzzle pieces.

_____   _____   _____
Category 1   Category 2   Category 3

Rearrange the words into different categories.

_____   _____   _____
Category 4   Category 5   Category 6

Sort and Show

Vocabulary Words

1.	5.	9.
2.	6.	10.
3.	7.	11.
4.	8.	12.

How do the words above fit together? Arrange them into three categories.

Label: ....

Label: ....

Label: ....

Vocabulary words:

Other words that fit in this category:

Vocabulary words:

Other words that fit in this category:

Vocabulary words:

Other words that fit in this category:

Words that fit into more than one category:	Categories:

9

Collective Nouns

Skill: *Learn that collective nouns represent groups of people, places, or things, and that these nouns may be used in either a singular or plural form*

Overview

Although students may not know the definition of *collective noun*, they are familiar with a number of these words. Common collective nouns include *board*, *jury*, *audience*, and *majority*. Less well known are *pride* (of lions), *colony* (of penguins), and *warren* (of rabbits). As students expand their vocabularies, they need to become familiar with collective nouns and their meanings. Not only do unusual collective nouns enrich student language, but many of them, such as *pride* and *board*, have multiple meanings, and knowing the meaning in the collective-noun context gives students more word power.

Collective nouns can be confusing when we try to decide whether they are singular or plural. Here is a rule of thumb to share with students: If the group is acting together, the verb, and any pronoun that refers to the collective noun, is singular; for example, *The polls show that the public is backing the incumbent.* If members of the group act as individuals, the verb, and any pronoun that refers to the collective noun, is plural, as in *The public do not agree about spending money for medical research.* Political science and government are two areas of the curriculum that lend themselves to the instruction of collective nouns.

How to Teach

The graphic organizers offered here should be used as students encounter collective nouns in their reading. You might want to highlight collective nouns with high-interest picture books focusing on collective nouns, such as Ruth Heller's *A Cache of Jewels*. This book supports vocabulary acquisition with illustrations of a bunch of bananas, a batch of bread, a kindle of kittens, and so on.

To target some of the collective nouns that will enrich students' daily and academic vocabularies, teach a mini-lesson that prepares

students for the graphic organizers in this lesson. Begin by explaining that a collective noun represents a group of people, places, or things, and then use common collective nouns as examples. Discuss the following: *It takes more than one baseball, football, or basketball player to make a team. There is an ant on the sidewalk, but a colony in the anthill.* Challenge students to find the collective nouns in the sentences (*team, colony*).

Create a list on the board with the following words (or list other collective nouns that your class knows): *herd, flock, class, family, audience.* Have students work with partners to brainstorm associated words for each noun. Have volunteers state their associations, and list them near the collective noun. Your completed board may look something like this:

Herd	sheep, cattle, cows
Flock	birds, chickens,
Class	all of us, high, middle, low
Family	father, mother and kids; mother and child; grandparents and children
Audience	people watching a show, play, movie

Discuss collective nouns in the singular form, acting as a group, as in *The Ortiz family has enough members to form its own softball team.* Compare this example to a sentence in which a collective noun is used as a plural form, when members of a group act as individuals. For example: *A family of ducks waddle one by one across the road, their tails swinging left and right.* Repeat this procedure with another example of a singular collective noun: *The audience keeps cheering, hoping it can bring the band back for another song.* Then, contrast this with the plural form of *audience*: *The audience of very young children were fidgeting, whispering, and giggling, much to their teachers' dismay.*

Have students continue the activity using the remaining words, in this case, *flock, class,* and *herd.*

Using the Tiered Organizers

When students understand that a collective noun represents a group but may be used in either the singular or plural form, they are ready to do one of the following graphic organizers.

Introductory: **Nouns by the Numbers**

Students use pictures to represent the difference between a group acting as a single unit and group members acting individually. They then write sentences using collective nouns in both plural and singular forms.

Intermediate: **Collective Comparisons**

Students identify two collective nouns, define them, and write sentences in which a collective noun is used in the singular and plural forms.

Challenging: **Collective Connections**

Students identify three collective nouns, define them, and write journal entries from the perspective of a collector, using the collective nouns in the correct singular or plural forms.

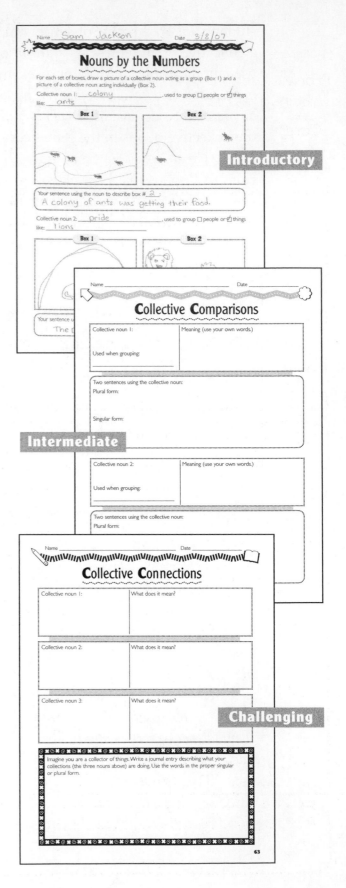

Nouns by the Numbers

For each set of boxes, draw a picture of a collective noun acting as a group (Box 1) and a picture of a collective noun acting individually (Box 2).

Collective noun 1: _____, used to group ☐ people or ☐ things

like: _____

Box 1	Box 2

Your sentence using the noun to describe box #_____.

Collective noun 2: _____, used to group ☐ people or ☐ things

like: _____

Box 1	Box 2

Your sentence using the noun to describe box #_____:

Collective Comparisons

Collective noun 1:

Used when grouping:

_____

Meaning (use your own words.)

Two sentences using the collective noun:

Plural form:

Singular form:

Collective noun 2:

Used when grouping:

_____

Meaning (use your own words.)

Two sentences using the collective noun:

Plural form:

Singular form:

Collective Connections

Collective noun 1:	What does it mean?

Collective noun 2:	What does it mean?

Collective noun 3:	What does it mean?

Imagine you are a collector of things. Write a journal entry describing what your collections (the three nouns above) are doing. Use the words in the proper singular or plural form.

10

Affixes

Skill: *Explore ways in which prefixes and suffixes change a base word's meaning or part of speech*

Overview

According to an analysis conducted by White, Sowell, and Yanigihara (1989), 11 prefixes account for 81% of all prefixed words and six suffixes account for 80% of all suffixed words. Stahl (2005) calls these "high-leverage prefixes and suffixes" and they are the ones to target in vocabulary instruction. As we teach students to recognize these affixes and understand their impact on word meaning, we provide our students with the tools they need to access a wide range of new vocabulary.

How to Teach

Explain (or review) the difference between base words and root words. Base words, such as *happy* or *new*, are words that can either stand alone or be added to, in order to alter the meaning (*unhappy, newness*). Define *affixes* as word elements added to the beginning or end of base words to change the meaning or part of speech of the words; prefixes attach to the beginnings of words while suffixes attach to the ends. Some common affixes are prefixes, such as *re-* or *un-*; some are suffixes, such *-ed*, or *-tion*. When teaching affixes, focus on either prefixes or suffixes. In this prefix lesson, we focus on *semi-*, *mid-*, and *pre-*.

On the board or overhead, create a two-column chart with columns A and B. List *semicircle*, *semiconscious*, and *semiannual* in Column A. Identify each base word (*circle, conscious, annual*) and write it in Column B. Have students determine what Column A words have in common. Prompt them to deduce that the prefix *semi-* can mean "half, part, or once every half." Provide a few other examples and then invite students to brainstorm other words that contain the prefix *semi-*. Continue to record answers on the chart. Repeat this process with the prefixes *mid-* and *pre-*. Discuss why these three prefixes might be studied in the same lesson (these prefixes signal temporal relationships—based on time). Keep in mind as you introduce new

vocabulary that affixes with common meanings should be grouped together for instruction.

Be prepared for students to suggest some words that don't fit the pattern: Students may suggest words that begin with the letter groups *semi* or *pre*, but do not follow the pattern of prefix and base word, such as *seminary* or *prefer*. Remind students that there must be a base word on which to attach the prefix—otherwise what appears to be a prefix may simply be part of the word.

Next, talk about situations in which you might use some of the words from Column A. Say, for example, "I might use *semiconductor* if I were talking about electrical circuits." Model another word, using the same process. Next, ask students to define the remaining words in Column A and to suggest situations in which each word might be used. Have students review what they know about prefixes (or suffixes) that they have been studying in this lesson.

Using the Tiered Organizers

When students can identify base words and affixes, match each student with the appropriate tiered activity.

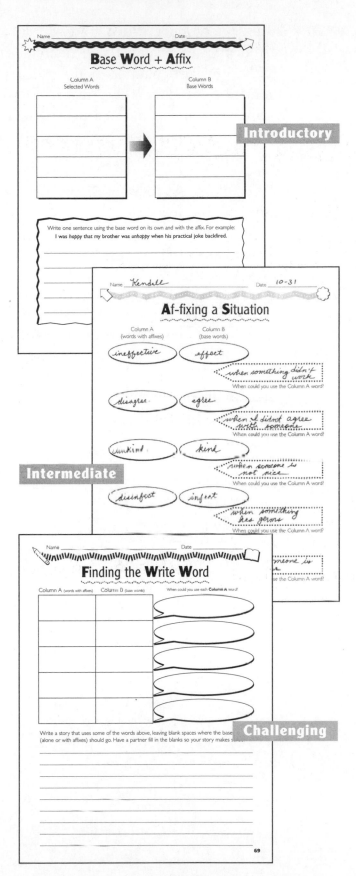

Introductory: **Base Word + Affix**

Students locate words that contain target prefixes or suffixes in books across the curriculum, or you may want to give them a list. They create a word chart of their own, recording words they find in Column A and base words in Column B. Challenge students to apply the meaning of the base word on its own and with the affix by using them both in one sentence.

Intermediate: **Af-fixing a Situation**

Students locate words that contain target prefixes or suffixes in books across the curriculum, or you may want to give them a list. They create a word chart of their own, recording words they find in Column A and base words in Column B. To the right of Column B, students can provide situations in which they might use the words.

Challenging: **Finding the Write Word**

Students complete the same activities in *Af-fixing a Situation.* In addition, students write a story, leaving blank spaces where a base word or base word with an affix appears. Students then give the story to a partner, who fills in the blanks so that the story makes sense.

Base Word + Affix

Column A Selected Words		Column B Base Words

Write one sentence using the base word on its own and with the affix. For example:

I was *happy* that my brother was *unhappy* when his practical joke backfired.

_____

_____

_____

_____

_____

Af-fixing a **S**ituation

Column A
(words with affixes)

Column B
(base words)

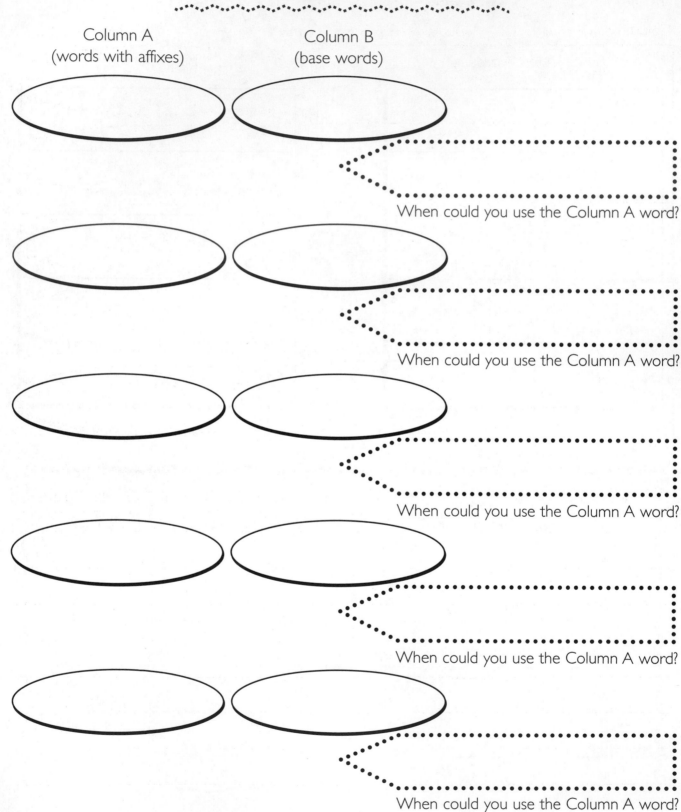

When could you use the Column A word?

When could you use the Column A word?

When could you use the Column A word?

When could you use the Column A word?

When could you use the Column A word?

Finding the Write Word

Column A (words with affixes)	Column B (base words)	When could you use each **Column A** word?

Write a story that uses some of the words above, leaving blank spaces where the base words (alone or with affixes) should go. Have a partner fill in the blanks so your story makes sense.

_____

_____

_____

_____

_____

_____

_____

_____

Latin Roots

Skill: *Use Latin roots to unlock meaning for a variety of words*

Overview

Latin and Greek roots can be a vehicle for getting at the gist of meaning for a large number of words. Dictionaries often show that although English usage comes from a French, German, or Italian word, many of our words have Latin or Greek origins. By learning Latin roots, students can make an educated guess about a word's meaning, and with the help of context clues, understand even more. (See Chapter 12 for Greek roots.)

How to Teach

It is best to teach Latin roots that are most commonly found in material your students are currently reading. This lesson focuses on six common Latin roots, highlighted in the chart on page 71, but you may want to substitute others for your own instruction.

Begin the lesson by explaining the meaning of the first root in the list: *aud*, which means "hear." (You may want to point out that unlike base words, which can stand alone and still have full meaning (*physics*), roots are meaningful units, like *geo*, which must be attached to other word parts, including base words and affixes, to form a complete word (*geophysics, geology*). Ask students if they know any words that include the root *aud*. You may get suggestions that do not apply, such as *auditor*, but students should be able to come up with words like *audience, auditorium,* and *audition*. Discuss each word and its relationship to the root *aud*. Prompt students to name other words associated in some way with hearing, and point out the ones that include the root *aud*. Discuss how each word might be used, who might use it, and where it might be used. Repeat this procedure with the other five roots.

Latin Roots	Meaning	Word Examples
aud	hear	auditory, audience, audible, audition, auditorium
fin	end, limit	final, finite, finish, finally, finale, finalist, finalize
port	carry	export, import, portable, porter, portfolio, deport, deportation
quest	seek, ask	question, quest, questionnaire
sen	feel, think	sensory, sensitive, sensation, sense, sensibility, sensor, sentiment
rupt	break	disrupt, interrupt, rupture, corrupt, corruption, interruption, disruption

Using the Tiered Organizers

Students are ready to work with one of the graphic organizers when they recognize that many English words may stem from one Latin root. Along with the graphic organizers, give students a list of Latin roots they should keep an eye out for in their readings.

Introductory: **Rooting for Words**
Students write a Latin root and its meaning, and then use the dictionary or other sources to find words that stem from this root. They explain how the meaning of the root is connected to the meaning of the discovered

words. Finally, they illustrate two of the word meanings.

Intermediate: **Growing From Roots**
Students write a Latin root and its meaning, and then use the dictionary or other sources to find other words that stem from this root. Next, they explain how the meaning of the root is connected to the meaning of the discovered words, and how each new word could be used. Finally, they use two of the new words in one sentence using the application explained in the chart.

Challenging: **Latin Limbs**
Students write a Latin root and its meaning, and then use the dictionary and other sources to find words that stem from this root. They explain how the meaning of the root is connected to the meaning of the discovered words, and how each new word could be used, who would use it, and where it might be used. Finally, they use two of the new words in sentences that express the meanings of the words.

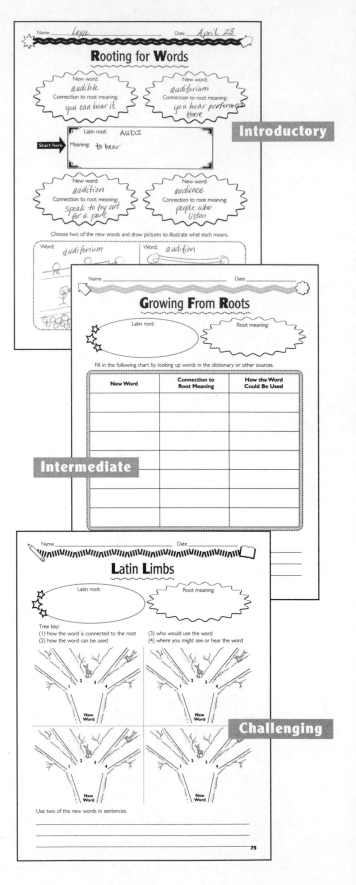

Rooting for Words

New word:

Connection to root meaning:

New word:

Connection to root meaning:

Start here →

Latin root:

Meaning:

New word:

Connection to root meaning:

New word:

Connection to root meaning:

Choose two of the new words and draw pictures to illustrate what each means.

Word:

Word:

Name _____ Date _____

Growing From Roots

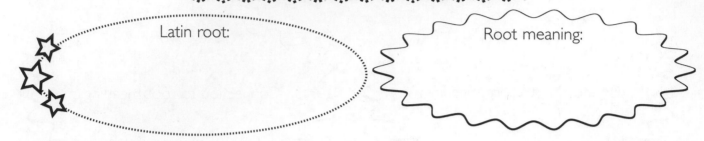

Latin root: _____

Root meaning: _____

Fill in the following chart by looking up words in the dictionary or other sources.

New Word	Connection to Root Meaning	How the Word Could Be Used

Use two of the new words in one sentence.

_____

_____

_____

Latin Limbs

Latin root:

Root meaning:

Tree key:
(1) how the word is connected to the root
(2) how the word can be used

(3) who would use the word
(4) where you might see or hear the word

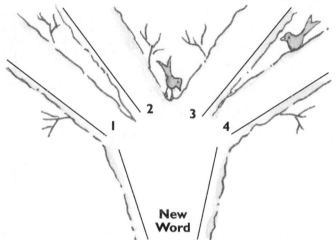

2 3
1   4

New Word

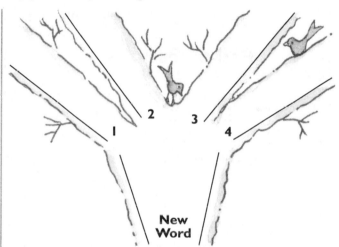

2 3
1   4

New Word

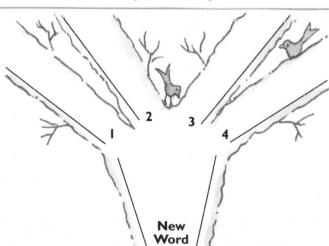

2 3
1   4

New Word

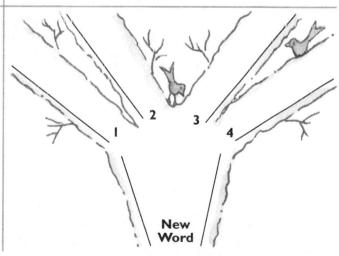

2 3
1   4

New Word

Use two of the new words in sentences.

_____

_____

_____

Greek Roots

Skill: *Use Greek roots to unlock the meaning of a variety of words*

Overview

Knowing the meaning of a root can unlock the meanings of many related words. In Chapter 11, Latin Roots, you will find more background and ideas on teaching basic etymology through root word instruction.

How to Teach

Begin by comparing and contrasting roots, base words, and affixes (see chapters 10 and 11). Share four examples of familiar roots from the worlds of science and math that are of Greek origin. For example: *therm* (heat), *bi* (two), *mega* (great), and *bio* (life).

Divide chart paper into four blocks. Print one root at the top of each box and have students brainstorm three or four words containing that root and list them in each box. Read aloud the words in each box and have students deduce what each root means. Write the root's meaning in the box, using a different colored marker. Review the listed words and ask students to define them, using their knowledge of the root to support each meaning. Record their answers. When the class disagrees about or is unsure of an answer, have students consult a dictionary. Have students discuss connections between the words and their own experiences.

It's important to reinforce the roots by using them in meaningful contexts. Model sentences that contain words with the Greek roots you're studying (see examples below). Begin sentences with "I wonder…" Be sure the meaning of each new word is clear in the sentence.

I wonder how long the soup in my thermos bottle would remain hot if I kept the top off the bottle.

I wonder if it's better to get paid every week, or to get paid biweekly.

I wonder if most scientists got A's in biology when they were in high school.

I wonder if it's easier or harder to hear someone who is using a megaphone?

Have students offer sample sentences of their own or revise and improve your sentences to make the meaning even more evident.

Finally, using words with the Greek roots you've been practicing, write a catchy newspaper headline for an imaginary article. Explain what the article would be about. Your headline might read something like, *Megavirus Hits Computers* and you would explain that this article would be about a widespread, crippling computer virus. Pair students and have each set of partners create one headline and prepare to discuss what their article might be about. When partners have shared, but before they explain their headline, encourage the class to identify the Greek root and meaning of the target word.

Here is a list of additional Greek roots to help you teach this skill:

* Government: *dem* (people), *crac/crat* (rule or govern), *polis/polit* (city, state, citizen)

* Communication: *gram/graph* (write), *aud* (hear), *log* (speak), *phon* (sound or voice), *scope* (to see), *spec/spect/spic* (to look at or to behold)

* Prepositions: *endo/ento* (within), *peri* (around or about), *pre* (before)

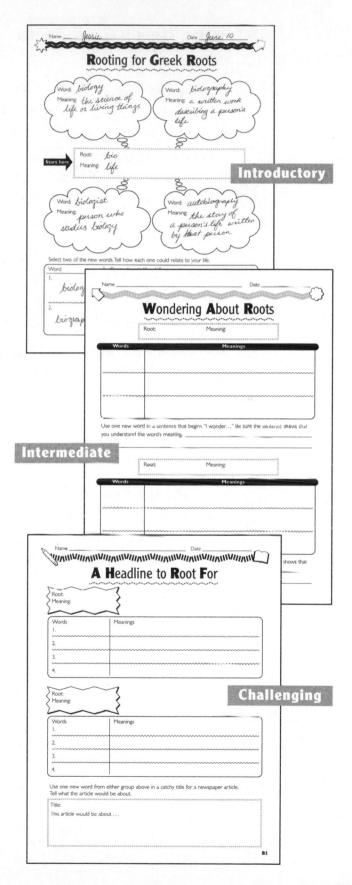

Using the Tiered Organizers

When students can identify words containing Greek roots, use their knowledge of roots to determine approximate meanings of unfamiliar words, and use the new words in context, match each student with an appropriate graphic organizer.

You can use the graphic organizers to reinforce one root with all of your students or assign different roots to different students. Students may also use texts they are reading and dictionaries to locate words that contain Greek roots or you may want to supply the words.

Introductory: **Rooting for Greek Roots**

Students identify one Greek root and its meaning. They make a web of related words and define each new word, then they select two new words and connect them to their own experience.

Intermediate: **Wondering About Roots**

Students identify a Greek root and write its meaning. They list words that contain this root, write definitions of the words, and use one word from the list in an "I wonder…" sentence, as shown in the model lesson. Sentences should demonstrate an understanding of the word's meaning. Finally, students repeat this procedure with a different Greek root.

Challenging: **A Headline to Root For**

Students identify two Greek roots and write their meanings. They list words that contain each root and write the definitions for the words. In addition, they create catchy headlines for imaginary newspaper articles, using words from their lists. Finally, they explain what the articles would be about.

Name _____ Date _____

Rooting for **G**reek **R**oots

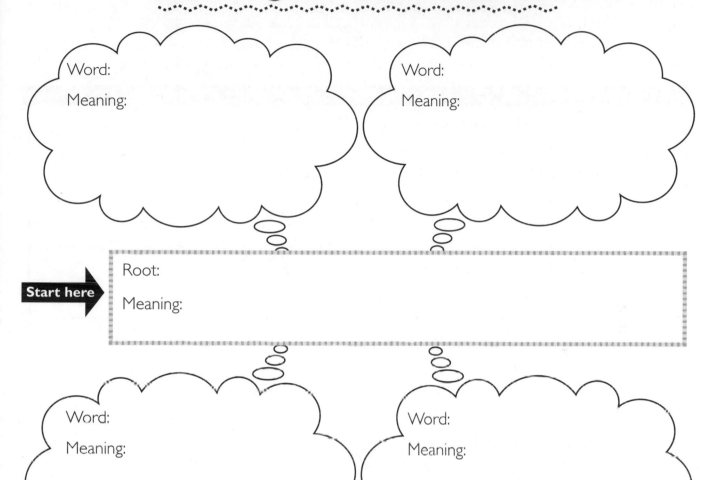

Word:

Meaning:

Word:

Meaning:

Start here →

Root:

Meaning:

Word:

Meaning:

Word:

Meaning:

Select two of the new words. Tell how each one could relate to your life.

Word	Connection to Your Life
1.	
2.	

Wondering About Roots

Root: _____ Meaning: _____

Words	Meanings

Use one new word in a sentence that begins, "I wonder…" Be sure the sentence shows that you understand the word's meaning. _____

_____

Root: _____ Meaning: _____

Words	Meanings

Use one new word in a sentence that begins, "I wonder…" Be sure the sentence shows that you understand the word's meaning. _____

_____

A Headline to Root For

Root:
Meaning:

Words	Meanings
1.	
2.	
3.	
4.	

Root:
Meaning:

Words	Meanings
1.	
2.	
3.	
4.	

Use one new word from either group above in a catchy title for a newspaper article.
Tell what the article would be about.

Title:

This article would be about . . .

Etymology: Word History

Skill: *Make use of word history to determine word meaning and usage*

Overview

Etymology is the study of word history. Learning word history is not only interesting, it also offers students another tool to help them recall the meanings of words. Take the word *milestone*, for instance. According to *In a Word: 750 Words and Their Fascinating Stories and Origins* (Baker, 2003)— a great resource written for students in grades 5 to 9—*milestone* originated during the Roman Empire. Along Roman roads, a stone marker was placed about every 1,000 paces (nearly a mile in length) and the distance to the Forum in Rome was chiseled into the stone. Over the years, *milestone* has come to mean "an important point or event in a person's life."

Good dictionaries give an abbreviated form of word history, including Latin or Greek roots (these topics are presented on pages 70–81). However, word history books like Baker's go into greater detail, describing how words pass from one culture into another, changing slightly in the process, and evolving into the words we use today. For example, the word *applaud* comes from the Latin verb *plaudere* (to strike or beat); later, Romans added the prefix *ad-*, meaning "to." Over time, through general use in the English language *applaudite* was shortened to *applaud* (Baker, 2003). Another example of a word that has changed over time is *picnic*, which has evolved from the French word *piquenique*, meaning "outing for food."

How to Teach

Highlighting and discussing words from students' reading is a wonderful way to begin a lesson on word history. Choose words that you know have an interesting background (confirm with a dictionary or with books on etymology). For example, in the novel *Someone Was Watching* (Patneaude, 1993), the word *depot* is used to refer to a train station. Write the word on the board, with the pronunciation (*dee-po*). Tell your class that many French words and names include a final, silent *t*, like *Monet*, and that

you think *depot* may come from a French word. Show that the dictionary confirms your suspicion. The dictionary also shows that the French word *depost* came from the Latin word *depositum*, meaning "deposit." Write *depost* and *depositum* on the board and discuss how the spelling of the word has changed. Explain that in English, *depot* can mean "train station" or "a place to store things," as in the military expression, *weapons depot*. Ask students why they think many super stores have chosen *depot* as part of their store name. They may tell you that it suggests a place where you'll find everything you need.

As another example, write the word *recite* on the board. The dictionary reveals that this word came from the French word *reciter*, which derives from the Latin word *recitare*, meaning "to call or cite." Then ask students if they know the contemporary meaning of *recite* (to recall and speak from memory).

Explain that the dictionary provides notes on the etymology, or history, of words. Give students dictionaries to share and have them look up the word *bizarre*. Show how the origin of *bizarre* may be found at the beginning or end of the list of meanings and point out that sometimes the dictionary will show more than one origin (*bizarre*

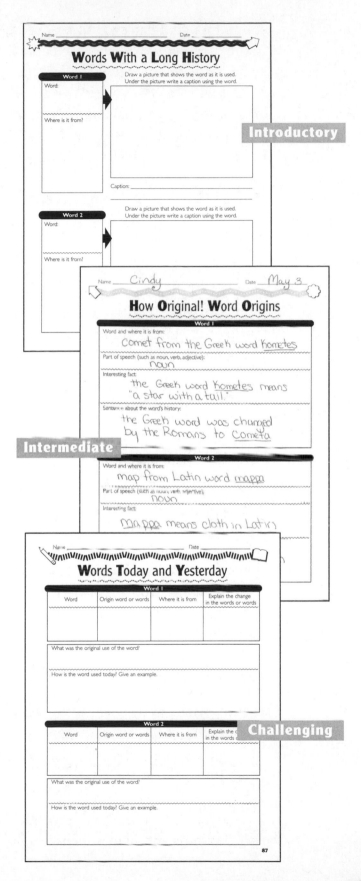

shows French, Spanish, and Basque derivations). Also discuss the symbols in the dictionary that label the parts of speech. Do the same with all or some of the following words: *cork, herb, chorus,* and *idiot,* listing them on a chart with the categories: Word, Language(s) of Origin, Parts of Speech, and Meanings, and having students volunteer answers to fill in the chart. Students should be comfortable looking at the origin(s) and parts of speech prior to doing the graphic organizers.

Using the Tiered Organizers

Students are ready to work with one of the following graphic organizers when they understand that words have historical origins from which current meanings have evolved, and can locate relevant information in the dictionary.

To complete these graphic organizers, students need a variety of lexicons: dictionaries, word history books, and online resources. We recommend Rosalie Baker's *In a Word*, Mary Jo Fresch and Aileen Wheaton's *The Spelling List and Work Study Resource Book*, and *The Merriam-Webster New Book of Word Histories*.

The graphic organizers offered here can be used in two ways. They may be used to help students remember meanings as they encounter new words in their reading, or they can become an independent activity to help students enlarge their vocabularies. Students can pick an interesting word from a dictionary or other source, and fill out the graphic organizer with the word.

Introductory: **Words With a Long History**
Students write two words and their origins, and then draw pictures that put the words in context. Under the pictures they write captions using the words.

Intermediate: **How Original! Word Origins**
Students write two words and their origins, parts of speech, and an interesting fact about each word. Then students use each word in a sentence about the word's history.

Challenging: **Words Today and Yesterday**
Students write two words and their origins and note how the words have changed from their original form. They also write how the words were used historically, and how they are used currently.

Words With a Long History

Word 1

Word:

_____

Where is it from?

Draw a picture that shows the meaning of the word.
Under the picture write a caption using the word.

Caption: _____

Word 2

Word:

_____

Where is it from?

Draw a picture that shows the meaning of the word.
Under the picture write a caption using the word.

Caption: _____

_____

How Original! Word Origins

Word 1

Word and where it is from:

Part of speech (such as noun, verb, adjective):

Interesting fact:

Sentence about the word's history:

Word 2

Word and where it is from:

Part of speech (such as noun, verb, adjective):

Interesting fact:

Sentence about the word's history:

Words Today and Yesterday

Word 1

Word	Origin word or words	Where it is from	Explain the change in the words or words

What was the original use of the word?

How is the word used today? Give an example.

Word 2

Word	Origin word or words	Where it is from	Explain the change in the words or words

What was the original use of the word?

How is the word used today? Give an example.

14

Words Borrowed From Other Languages

Skill: *Employ words borrowed from other languages in order to flavor and enhance vocabulary*

Overview

It is amazing how many words we have borrowed from other languages—common ones like *pizza, bagel* and even *yo*—and more unusual words, such as *bon voyage, chutzpah,* and *kowtow*. Using words borrowed from other languages gives students, savoir-faire, or know-how. It flavors their oral and written speech and improves their understanding of the increasingly sophisticated texts they read.

Although you'll want to take vocabulary words from texts students read, start with the model lesson offered here to raise students' awareness of "borrowed words" in the English language.

How to Teach

Write the following sentences on the board with the "borrowed words" underlined.

(1) *Clean your room right now, I mean presto!*

(2) *Since your parents are out of town, your aunt may sign the field trip permission slip in loco parentis.*

(3) *Sayonara, Jess! I need to leave, so I'll see you tomorrow.*

Explain that English borrows many words from other languages and that some of these words are so widely used in speech and print that they are listed in English dictionaries. Offer familiar examples of English words with Spanish origins, such as *adios, taco,* and *siesta*. Remind students that context can often help them understand words they don't know, and that this is also true with borrowed words. If context clues fail to provide a word's meaning, students should refer to a dictionary.

Next, bring students' attention to the sentences on the board. Go through each sentence individually, challenging students to determine the meaning of the unfamiliar term from the words surrounding it

(*presto* means "right now," *in loco parentis* means "in place of a parent," and *sayonara* means "goodbye"). Encourage students to describe ways in which they associate the word with their own experiences; for instance, the word *presto* may remind students of a time they had to get something done quickly. Then have students say or rewrite the sentence, replacing the borrowed word with a synonymous word or phrase: "Clean your room right now, I mean *immediately* (*right this minute, instantly, straight away*)!"

To culminate the lesson, have students discuss other words that may be "borrowed," and then have partners share their ideas with the class. Words that might come up include: *bouquet, tete-a-tete, mesa, bravo, enchilada, spaghetti, bon appetit, hola,* and *quahog* (a hard-shelled clam found in New England).

Using the Tiered Organizers

Students are ready to complete one of the following graphic organizers when they recognize that the English language borrows words from other languages, and that the meanings of these words can often be discerned from context.

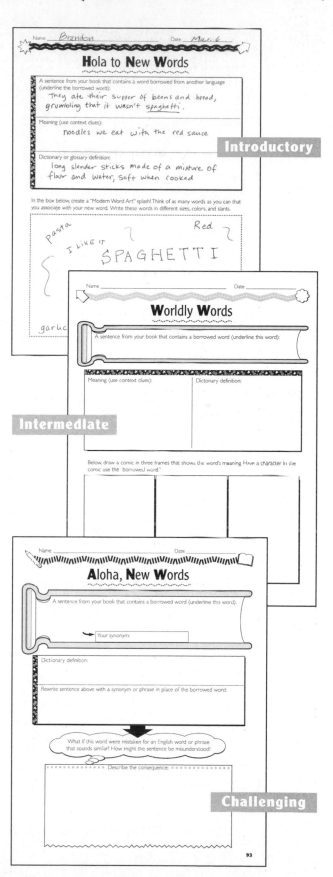

Introductory: **Hola to New Words**

Students choose a sentence from their reading that contains a word borrowed from another language. They write the sentence, what they think the meaning is, and the word's dictionary definition. Then they create a collage using words they associate with the "borrowed word."

Intermediate: **Worldly Words**

Students choose a sentence from their reading that contains a word borrowed from another language. Students write the sentence and underline the borrowed word. Then they write their own definition and the dictionary definition, and create a three-panel comic using the word.

Challenging: **Aloha, New Words**

Students choose a sentence from their reading that contains a word borrowed from another language. They write the sentence, underline the borrowed word, and write a definition for the word. Next, students rewrite the sentence, substituting another word phrase for the borrowed word. Students then give a nonexample by writing what could have happened if the "borrowed word" was misunderstood.

Hola to **N**ew **W**ords

A sentence from your book that contains a word borrowed from another language (underline the borrowed word):

Meaning (use context clues):

Dictionary or glossary definition:

In the box below, create a "Modern Word Art" splash! Think of as many words as you can that you associate with your new word. Write these words in different sizes, colors, and slants.

Worldly Words

A sentence from your book that contains a borrowed word (underline this word):

Meaning (use context clues):	Dictionary definition:

Below, draw a comic in three frames that shows the word's meaning. Have a character in the comic use the "borrowed word."

Aloha, New Words

A sentence from your book that contains a borrowed word (underline this word):

→ Your synonym:

Dictionary definition:

Rewrite sentence above with a synonym or phrase in place of the borrowed word:

What if this word were mistaken for an English word or phrase that sounds similar? How might the sentence be misunderstood?

Describe the consequence:

15

Modern Words

Skill: *Understand and be conscious of language growth and change*

Overview

Every year, there is hoopla as new words are entered in the Webster's or the American Heritage Dictionary. New words like *blog* are introduced, old words like *buggy whip* eventually disappear, or their meanings change—and so does our language.

As life gets more complicated, technology expands and science brings new discoveries, along with new words to describe them: *nanosecond, mp3 player, gigabyte*. Another influx of words comes from our youth culture. Adolescents give birth to their own teenspeak, which ends up in mainstream English. Words such as *dis* (put someone down) and *heelies* (shoes with wheels on the heels) infiltrate everyday speech. And just as new words are being created, old words change in meaning as they are used differently, often during informal speech. For example, the word *caboose* has traditionally the last car on the train but modern trains do not have cabooses, so most kids have never seen one. One child recently defined caboose as "the kid at the end of the line," so the term lives on, in a new context.

Working with words helps students see that our language is evolving and that they are active language users and innovators.

How to Teach

To cultivate an awareness in your classroom that language is a living, evolving mechanism for communication, review the following words and their meanings. Explain that these words did not always exist, but came into use through changes in modern life and human practices. The first two words, *Kleenex* and *Jello*, are actually brand names that have come to signify the products they sell. Everyone asks for a Kleenex, no matter the brand and no one ever asks for gelatin for dessert! These two words evolved after the invention of disposable handkerchiefs and gelatin was packaged as a flavored food product.

The next two words, *blog* and *blook*, are technology-related. The final word, *unibrow*, evolved from popular slang.

Kleenex: disposable paper handkerchief

Jello: flavored gelatin food

blog: a "web log" (hence '*blog*) posted on the Internet for everyone to read, and usually updated frequently

blook: cross between a blog and a book; blogs with fictional stories have been termed *blooks*, and some of these have been published in traditional formats

unibrow: eyebrows that appear to grow together because of hair growing between them

condexes: a house with two apartments, sold condominium style, which entails a condo fee and community property.

Go over the words with students, one at a time. Discuss each word's background, how it evolved, and what it means. Have students make associations to help them recall the word's meaning. Discuss what the word is not; for instance, *Kleenex* is not a cloth handkerchief and *blog* is not a newspaper or a television newscast.

Using the Tiered Organizers

The following graphic organizers should be used with words that are relatively new to the language, either garnered from student reading or provided by the teacher. Students are ready to work with these graphic organizers when they understand that words evolve because of cultural change, including changes in popular use, slang, and new technology.

Introductory: **Welcome to New Words**
Students brainstorm a list of words new to the language and write their meanings, making associations to improve their recall.

Intermediate: **New-Fangled Words**
Students write a word that is new to the language, describe what it means, and explain how the word may have originated. Then, students create a billboard slogan using the word appropriately.

Challenging: **Innovative Vocabulary**
Students write a new word, describe what it means, and explain how the word's current usage may have come about. They then create an ad showing the new word's meaning and when someone should use it (show the context for the usage).

Welcome to New Words

Newborn Word list (2 years or younger)	Meanings	Associations

New-Fangled Words

Word: _____

In your own words, explain what the word means:

How did the word originate?

In the box below, create a billboard slogan using the new word.

Innovative **V**ocabulary

The new word _____

What the word means:

The word's origin:

Imagine you are designing a two-sided ad for the new word on which pictures and text can be printed. On one side use the new word to show customers the meaning and origin of the word. On the other, show or tell when someone should use it.

Ad (side 1)

Ad (side 2)

Acronyms

Skill: *Make use of and understand acronyms, words formed from the first letters of other words*

Overview

Acronyms are words formed from the first letters of several words of a compound term, such as *radar* (radio detection and ranging). Freeman and Freeman (2004, p. 181) note that the word *acronym* comes from the Greek base *acro*, meaning "high," and *onym*, meaning "name." Acronyms are "high names," because they are created from capital letters, which are the tallest. Studying acronyms is an exciting way for students to discover how new words are born, as well as a valuable tool for recalling information in their learning across the curriculum.

How to Teach

Show several examples of acronyms taken from sources like novels and news articles your students may be reading. For instance, in the book *Hoot* (Hiaasen, 2002) one of the main characters, Mullet Finger, sees an older man go by and says, "He's got an ATV—it's super cool. Goes flyin' around here like he's Jeff Gordon" (page 174). Of course, we know ATV is an acronym for *all terrain vehicles*. Explain how acronyms are formed. Encourage students to offer acronyms they know, perhaps *asap* (as soon as possible), *rom* (read-only memory), *ram* (random access memory), or *scuba* (self-contained underwater breathing apparatus). Have students consider why people use acronyms. A Web search shows over 535,000 acronyms, many of which are content related or used to identify different organizations, such as NAFTA (North American Free Trade Agreement and North American Foreign Trade Association).

Next, explain that people sometimes use acronyms to help them remember and recall information (these kinds of memory tools are known as mnemonic devices). For example, people use the acronym *HOMES* to help them recall the names of the five Great Lakes: Huron,

Ontario, Michigan, Erie, and Superior. FARM B is an acronym that aids students in recalling the classification of vertebrates: fish, amphibians, reptiles, mammals, and birds.

Ask students to think of some acronyms that they may use in their daily lives. Point out that some of their examples are spelled out when spoken (initialism), while others are pronounced—both are acceptable forms of acronyms.

Common acronyms to share with your class include:

2D	two dimensional
AM	anti meridian (day)
PM	post meridian (night)
LOL	laugh out loud
4WD	four-wheel drive
SARS	Severe Acute Respiratory Syndrome
LNG	liquefied natural gas
TB	tuberculosis
TBA	to be announced
FYI	for your information
PE	physical education
AI	artificial intelligence
TNT	trinitro toluene
DVD	for digital video (or versatile) disc.

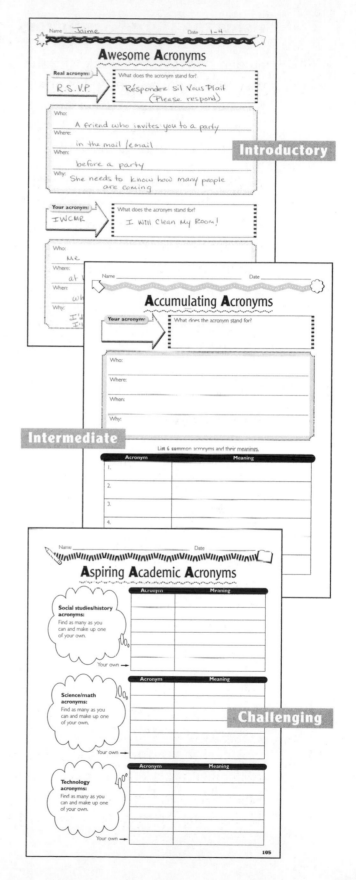

Using the Tiered Organizers

Students are ready to work with the graphic organizers when they can use the dictionary, a word history reference book (see Chapter 13), or the Internet to discover the meanings of acronyms and can create their own acronyms. As with all activities in this book, students should reconvene to share their findings when the activity is complete.

Introductory: **Awesome Acronyms**

The teacher or students name one common acronym. Students use a dictionary to find its meaning, then they record it. Next, students consider who might use this acronym, as well as where, when, and why it might be used. Then they create their own acronym and complete the second half of the organizer.

Intermediate: Accumulating Acronyms

Students create acronyms and identify who might use them, as well as where, when, and why they might be used. Students then list six common acronyms that would be familiar to most people.

Challenging: **Aspiring Academic Acronyms**

Students find, categorize, and define acronyms in the content areas (social studies/history, science/math, and technology). They then make up one acronym for each category and define it.

Awesome Acronyms

Real acronym:

What does the acronym stand for?

Who:

Where:

When:

Why:

Your acronym:

What does the acronym stand for?

Who:

Where:

When:

Why:

Accumulating Acronyms

Your acronym:

What does the acronym stand for?

Who:

Where:

When:

Why:

List 6 common acronyms and their meanings.

Acronym	Meaning
1.	
2.	
3.	
4.	
5.	
6.	

Aspiring Academic Acronyms

Social studies/history acronyms:

Find as many as you can and make up one of your own.

Acronym	Meaning
Your own ➤	

Science/math acronyms:

Find as many as you can and make up one of your own.

Acronym	Meaning
Your own ➤	

Technology acronyms:

Find as many as you can and make up one of your own.

Acronym	Meaning
Your own ➤	

Euphemisms

Skill: *Become familiar with polite words or phrases used to replace words that may be offensive*

Overview

According to *The Literacy Dictionary* (1995), a euphemism is a socially acceptable word or expression used in place of unacceptable or taboo language. The word *expecting* for *pregnant*, and the term *passed away* for *dead*, are examples of euphemisms. Euphemisms are often used when discussing sensitive topics such as weight and appearance, birth, death, income, religion, and politics. Because euphemisms are not literal expressions, they can be confusing, especially to English language learners.

How to Teach

Put the following words on the board: *fat*, *old person*, and *toilet*. Ask students how they might say each word or phrase in a more sensitive, less offensive way and list responses beside the words. Your list may look like this:

Word given	Euphemisms
fat	chubby, pleasingly plump, stout, portly, hefty, large
old person/old	senior citizen, pensioner, senior, seasoned, elderly
toilet	restroom, comfort station, john, WC (Water Closet), men's or women's room, washroom, lavatory

Discuss words one at a time. As students volunteer euphemisms, add others to the chart. Discuss differences between the euphemisms and the words they replace, and ask them to explain how the euphemisms change the tone of our language. Lead them to understand that the euphemism makes our language kinder and sometimes less offensive. Be aware that students may offer inappropriate language as euphemisms; for instance, for *fat*, someone may want to add *porker*, which is not a euphemism because it is a less sensitive, more offensive way of talking about someone who is fat. Remind students that a euphemism is used for its soothing influence, not to create conflict.

Write the following sentence on the board or overhead: *The old people went on a day trip to the canal.* Ask students how this sentence could be restated using a euphemism. Some acceptable answers are: *The senior citizens went on a day trip to the canal* or *The elderly people went on day trip to the canal.* Invite students to offer sentences that include some of the other euphemisms on the chart.

Discuss examples of euphemisms from literature students are reading. You may want to use for discussion the following sentence from E. L. Konigsburg's

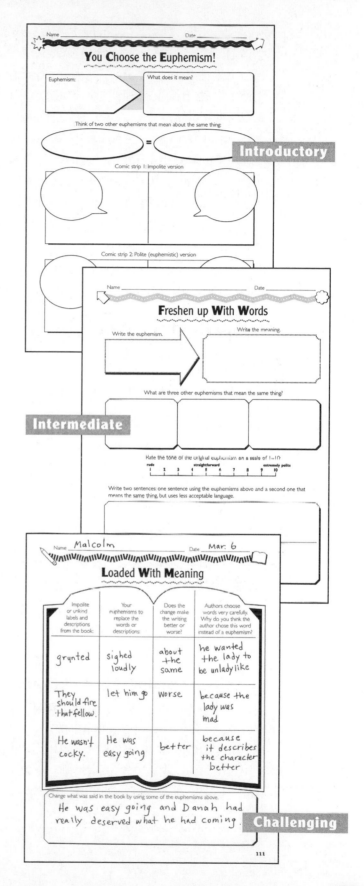

book *Jennifer, Hecate, Macbeth, William McKinley, and Me, Elizabeth*:
"In other words, my costume was a *hand-me-down* but Jennifer's was a
genuine *antique*." (page 7). Point out that the word *antique* puts a positive
spin on used clothing. Ask students to provide other euphemisms for a
hand-me-down, such as *vintage, gently used*, or *recycled clothing*. Have
students turn to page 9 in the book, where the main character gets a
detention and comments that the kids call it "staying after." In this case,
characters make up their own euphemism for a negative word.

Ask students to create their own euphemisms. Begin by asking
what euphemism they might use for *detention*. Then have the students
work in pairs to create euphemisms for other activities, events, or things
in their life that they dislike intensely, like those dreaded sprints in P.E.,
ugly school uniforms, and cafeteria food.

Using the Tiered Organizers

Students are ready to do one of the following graphic organizers when
they understand that euphemisms are acceptable words or phrases
used in place of unpleasant or offensive words.

Introductory: **You Choose the Euphemism**
Students write a euphemism, state its meaning, then offer two
synonymous euphemisms. They then draw one comic showing an
impolite way of expressing the euphemism and another polite version,
using the euphemism.

Intermediate: **Freshen up With Words**
Students write a euphemism and its meaning, give at least three
synonymous euphemisms, and using a scale, rate the tone of the
euphemism. Students create sentences both with and without
euphemistic language.

Challenging: **Loaded With Meaning**
Students find passages in their reading containing language that
could be expressed euphemistically. They write euphemisms that the
author might have used instead of the original language, and explain
why the author chose to use the words he or she did. Students then
rewrite the excerpt, replacing the harsh words with euphemisms.

You Choose the Euphemism!

Euphemism:

> What does it mean?

Think of two other euphemisms that mean about the same thing:

=

Comic strip 1: Impolite version

Comic strip 2: Polite (euphemistic) version

Freshen up With Words

Write the euphemism.

Write the meaning.

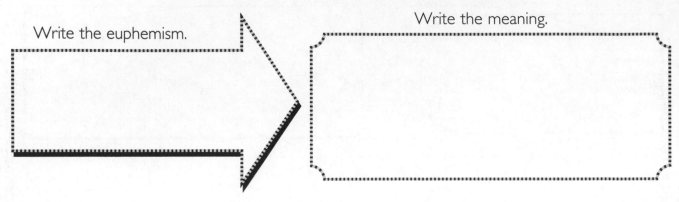

What are three other euphemisms that mean the same thing?

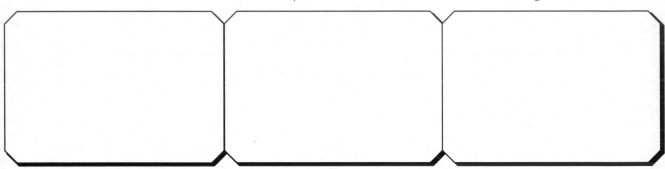

Rate the tone of the original euphemism on a scale of 1–10:

rude				straightforward				extremely polite	
1	2	3	4	5	6	7	8	9	10

Write two sentences: one sentence using the euphemisms above and a second one that means the same thing, but uses less acceptable language.

Loaded With Meaning

Impolite or unkind labels and descriptions from the book:	Your euphemisms to replace the words or descriptions:	Does the change make the writing better or worse?	Authors choose words very carefully. Why do you think the author chose this word instead of a euphemism?

Change what was said in the book by using some of the euphemisms above.

Children's Books Cited

Baker, R. F. (2003). *In a word: 750 words and their fascinating stories and origins*. Peterborough, NH: Cobblestone.

Carle, E. (2002). *Slowly, slowly, slowly said the sloth*. New York: Philomel Books.

Frasier, D. (2000). *Miss Alaineus, a vocabulary disaster*. New York: Harcourt.

Heller, R. (1987). *A cache of jewels*. New York: Grosset & Dunlap.

Hiaasen, C. (2002). *Hoot*. New York: Knopf Books for Young Readers.

Konigsburg, E. L. (2001). *Jennifer, Hecate, Macbeth, William McKinley and me, Elizabeth*. New York: Aladdin Paper Backs.

The Merriam-Webster New Book of Word Histories. (1995). Springfield, MA: Merriam-Webster.

Patneaude, David. (1993). *Someone was watching*. Morton Grove, IL: Albert Whitman and Co.

Sacher, Lois. (1998). *Holes*. New York: Farrar, Straus, and Giroux.

Snicket, L. (2004). *A series of unfortunate events*. New York: Scholastic, Inc.

Professional Works Cited

Adler, C. Ralph (Ed.), (2001). *Put Reading First*. The Partnership for Reading.

Baumann, J. F., Kame'enui, E. J., & Ash, G. E., (2003). Research on vocabulary instruction: Voltaire redux. In J. Flood, D. Lapp, J. R. Squire, and J.M. Jensen, *Handbook of research on teaching the English language arts (2nd ed.)* (pp.752-785). Mahwah, NJ: Lawrence Erlbaum Associates.

Beck, I., McKeown, M., & Kucan, L. (2002). *Bringing words to life: Robust vocabulary instruction*. NY: Guilford Press.

Block, C. C. (2005) "Powerful Vocabulary for Reading Success" Presentation given at Massachusetts Reading Association's Annual Conference. Sturbridge, MA.

Block, C. C., & Mangieri, J.N. (2005). *A research study to investigate the effects of The Powerful Vocabulary for Reading Success Program on Students' Reading Vocabulary and Comprehension Achievement* (Research report 2963-005 of the Institute for Literacy Enhancement). Scholastic Web Site.

Deasy, J. and Decker, J. (1990). *Field experience handbook in reading*, Unpublished paper. Bridgewater State College, Bridgewater, MA.

Frayer, D. A, Frederick, W. Ed., and Klausmeier, H. J. (1969). "A Schema for Testing the Level of Concept Mastery" (Working Paper #16). Madison, WI: Research and Development Center for Cognitive Learning.

Freeman, D. E., & Freeman, Y. S. (2004). *Essential linguistics: What you need to know to teach reading, ESL, spelling, phonics, and grammar.* Portsmouth, NH: Heinemann.

Fresch, M. J. & Wheaton, A. (2004). *The spelling list and word study resource book*. New York: Scholastic.

McKeown, M. (1985). The acquisition of word meaning from context by children of high and low ability. *Reading Research Quarterly, 20*, 482–496.

McKeown, M. G., Beck, I. L., Omansond, R. C., & Perfetti, C. A. (1983). The effects of long-term vocabulary instruction on reading comprehension: A replication. *Journal of Reading Behavior, 15*(1), 3–18.